Strategic
Error-Proofing

Strategic Error-Proofing

Achieving Success Every Time with Smarter FMEAs

John J. Casey

CRC Press is an imprint of the
Taylor & Francis Group, an **informa** business

A PRODUCTIVITY PRESS BOOK

Productivity Press
Taylor & Francis Group
270 Madison Avenue
New York, NY 10016

© 2009 by Taylor & Francis Group, LLC
Productivity Press is an imprint of Taylor & Francis Group, an Informa business

No claim to original U.S. Government works
Printed in the United States of America on acid-free paper
10 9 8 7 6 5 4 3 2 1

International Standard Book Number-13: 978-1-4200-8367-5 (Softcover)

Visit the Taylor & Francis Web site at
http://www.taylorandfrancis.com

and the Productivity Press Web site at
http://www.productivitypress.com

To My Wife Cindy,
the greatest person in the world for me.
And to our family who makes life complete.

Contents

Acknowledgments

I am so very thankful to all of the people who have helped me become a person who wants to pursue better ways and help other people grow. I also spend my days thankful for our son Tim, our daughter Amy, plus our daughter-in-law Erin, and our favorite dude Noah and favorite dudette Kate. My greatest teachers were my Mom and Dad. You'll never know the positive impact you have made on all of us (Kathy, Jim, and JoAnn). Thanks also to Marilyn, Jerry, Lisa, and Jon.

While writing this book, I was so very lucky to exchange ideas with a number of people, especially Scott Garberding for his vision and common sense. I also benefited greatly from Mark Wrobbel, a true quality professional who constantly looked to find solid methods to make the world of production a better place.

During the development of the concepts, I had the pleasure of talking to quite a number of people in the Quality Assurance and Audit Team, Roger Ruggiero, Gene Aldrich, Jeff Bobcean, Gregg Neale, Kim Fleming, Jim Lenhardt, Jim Hare, Kurt Vogler, D'Anna Keeble, Ping Zhang, Anna Cierpial, Jeff Gordon, Todd Anderson, Dave Hartz, Frank Macco, Damon Davie, Kelly Corrin, Ann Miller, Javier Zarazua, Andy Ly, John Lacks, Ken Simpson, and Leslie Michael. The exchange of ideas and the pursuit of the highest standard, like we frequently said, "Ha, ha, ha, this is great, let's kick it up another notch—Bool-yah!" We must always be pursuing a better way.

In addition, a few people said words or made suggestions that stimulated a better idea. Greg Deveson had a great way to describe the pursuit of the simplest method, using a term "I want to drive creativity before we spend capital." I also want to acknowledge Russell Williams and Chris Estock as two people who helped me and others find means to make the process simple and complete.

I also want to thank Tere Stouffer for her tireless editing and revising of the book plus Michael Sinocchi for having the confidence in me to pull the book together.

On a final note, I want to thank the thousands and thousands of people in the auto industry that work so hard every day to make great products for the world. The industry is in transition, the challenges are real, we need to keep pushing to achieve Success Every Time. Let's get SET for the next century!

Introduction

The auto industry has made terrific gains in quality over the past twenty-five years. Most of it came with the Toyota Production System (TPS) and the tenets of lean manufacturing, but regardless of the reason, the cars and trucks on the market are far better than they have ever been before: they have more features; they are less expensive on an inflation-adjusted basis; and they are far more reliable. This goes for any car made by any company. Every company has gotten the message, and most are chasing every angle possible in order to reduce costs by improving quality. It truly is a great time to be an automotive *consumer.*

But being an automotive *manufacturer* is a different story. The industry is in a restructuring mode, and a new, competitive landscape is emerging. Competition is intense, especially from new players, like the emerging car market in India, where wages are substantially lower, there's no retirement/pension system, and healthcare benefits are much less expensive, if they exist at all. Established auto manufacturers tend to be locked into a fixed-cost structure that jeopardizes their competitiveness.

That's why the pursuit of quality makes so much sense. When you produce more efficiently and have fewer defects, less rework, and less scrap, you have huge cost savings. If your products are better and you have fewer warranty claims, you get happier customers and less cost of replacement parts and repairs. Quality is definitely the smartest thing you could ever focus on if you are a corporation that wants to win. But you already know all of this, because every manufacturer, whether in the auto industry or not, is facing similar pressure.

In the auto industry, we have a method to help you avoid what is wrong. Failure Mode Effects Analysis (FMEA) looks for failure modes and their effects and gives you a way to analyze the situations and help you reduce your risk. It's quite a good method to help you learn from your past mistakes. You can take any problem, analyze it, find a way to better protect the customer, write that new method down, and avoid the same problem in the future.

Unfortunately, FMEA is not a method to help you do more of what is right; it is a method to help you avoid what can go wrong. What about a method to help things go right? Perhaps there are a few items you may be thinking can help operators have their operations "go right." The first might be standardized work instructions, including ones that are rich with pictures. It's true that work instructions help operators understand how a job is designed, but work instructions cannot guide the hands of operators. You may also be thinking about design for six sigma or design for manufacturing. These, too, are great approaches but at the point of production on every single piece, they do not put into place an error-proofing system.

With defect rates under 200 parts per million, many companies are chasing needles in haystacks, which is why low cost, strategic error-proofing devices are required to achieve the performance that differentiates you from your competitors. You need a logical approach to help operators do each job and do it correctly every time. You need to deploy error-proofing devices strategically and proactively to help your operators succeed.

Success Every Time (SET) is a structured methodology to establish a production environment where operators are strategically set up to succeed, all day, every day, thereby increasing first time yield and profits. SET stacks the deck for your operators, so that they can *only* succeed. When SET is executed completely, failure is not an option. Think of the bumpers they put in the gutters of the bowling alley when children are learning to bowl. If the ball goes off center, the bumpers push the ball into the proper area. They help do things right by forcing an automatic correction *before* the mistake is made and noticed. The bumpers stack the deck so the bowler cannot throw a gutter ball, which is one level of success. If you take the SET process a little further, you could also design the lane to be on an incline so that gravity can help the bowler get the speed needed to hit the pins. And so on.

SET, therefore, is a step-by-step method for implementing a production system in which production operators can *only* succeed. The operators interface with their parts and tools in such a way that either the product is made correctly, or the product/process is stopped. Operators can make only good parts—nothing else. For this reason, proper implementation of SET drives higher first time yield, increases customer satisfaction, improves warranty claims, improves profits, and helps you compete.

If you have been involved in quality and are familiar with FMEA, keep in mind that SET is the *inverse* of FMEA. Instead of failures, you focus on doing things right. Instead of control and detection, you focus on structured actions and allowing value-added operations to function only when every-thing is exactly right. Whereas FMEA drives low-risk priority numbers, SET drives high numbers. SET however, does utilize the greatest asset of FMEA, which is a logical and methodical approach.

SET Versus Strategic Error-Proofing

The terms *Success Every Time* (SET) and *strategic error-proofing* mean roughly the same thing. I prefer the term *SET,* however, because "error-proofing" is often used incorrectly in manufacturing as a synonym for mistake-proofing, FMEA, or poke-yoke (see Chapter 1 for details on these terms). So, in this book, I use SET to refer to the entire approach, one that uses *error-proofing devices* as one part of a strategy (see Chapter 10).

Consider this analogy: if you want to lose weight, you might decide to take an aerobics class three times per week. With these workouts, you will have some success, and you will lose weight. However, if you complement exercise with better foods, better sleep patterns, and other methods, you can lose weight faster and more permanently. Error-proofing is the exercise class, and SET is the com-plete weight loss plan.

SET can do all of the following at your facility:

■ SET defines a logic stream for engineers to strategically incorporate no-cost or low-cost error-proofing devices to help production operators.
■ SET shows how to integrate error-proofing devices into each value-add-ing activity to eliminate errors wherever possible.
■ SET identifies simple and strategic graphics to help management see improvements in elements that matter most, like safety and warranty claims.
■ SET outlines a method to measure the robustness of each operation as well as the plant overall.
■ SET attempts to maximize the returns of error-proofing devices in order to maximize profits.

This book helps you implement SET in your own facility, taking you through the process step-by-step.

■ In Chapter 1, which discusses some common terminology, you see that FMEAs have served companies well, but due to its fundamental approach to try to predict and control *all* possible failures, we have passed the point of diminishing returns. FMEAs are chasing infinity. In this chapter, I also look at how systematically utilizing poke-yoke devices—while recognizing the strategic difference between error-proofing and mistake-proofing—will improve your costs and profits.

■ In Chapter 2, you see how powerful quality can be in increasing your profits. Quality is the only activity that can simultaneously increase profits, customer satisfaction, productivity, and revenue. This chapter also establishes a foundation on how the SET method is a focused strategy that can achieve these ends.

■ The most compelling case for SET is the relatively few points of focus required to achieve success. For each operation, there are three categories of concentration. If you provide error-proofing devices for operators to succeed in these areas, you can raise your level of customer satisfaction significantly.

■ Every day, operators in your plant select parts, orient them properly, and place them precisely in a fixture before they take an action to impose some energy that adds the value to your products. Operators may perform these steps exactly right 9,998 times out of 10,000 and do the steps imperfectly only 2 times out of every 10,000. The SET method is seeking to provide cost-effective tools to reduce the 2 out of 10,000. Chapter 4 illustrates how the strategic placement of error-proofing devices drives up your profits and throughput. You are also introduced to the concept of a Success Likelihood Number that illustrates the degree of error-proofing support at each operation.

■ Your operators need their jobs to be set up properly before they even begin working on a manufactured unit. In Chapter 5, you discover how to monitor job set-ups, and see the influence the set-up process has in the Success Likelihood Number.

■ The third item in the critical elements you want to monitor is the value-added energy. After parts are placed exactly in the correct group of properly aligned tools and fixtures, the last step is to impart the exact amount of energy at the right location. This is the heart of Chapter 6. The chapter closes with a description of how to calculate the final Success Likelihood Number for each operation within a production line.

■ To achieve SET, you will be looking at individual component parts and testing your designs to make them easier to error-proof. Chapter 7 discusses simple and inexpensive ways to design parts that will respond well to error-proofing devices.

- When you make the decision to seek total customer satisfaction and you invest in strategic error-proofing devices, some critical factors are important to maximize the return on your investment. Chapter 8 illustrates the most powerful activities that can help you maximize your success.
- To achieve SET, you will be installing error-proofing devices, so an important question to ask is, "How can we determine how great a device is?" In Chapter 9, I help you answer this question and provide some simple and effective evaluation tools to rate your devices.
- SET a strategy. Chapter 10 outlines how the individual elements of SET work together to create a much stronger strategy that improves your competitiveness.
- Chapter 11 describes how everyone in your company can be linked in a SET method that pleases your customers, increases your throughput, lowers your operating costs, and increases your profits.

GETTING STARTED WITH SUCCESS EVERY TIME

Chapter 1

FMEA, Poke-Yoke, Mistake-Proofing, and Error-Proofing: Sorting Out the Terminology

The U.S. auto industry has been pursuing quality with a passion to stop things that could go wrong—that is, prevent issues and problems from reaching customers. This truly is a smart move. Unfortunately, it is being done in the "things gone wrong" method of Failure Mode Effects Analysis (FMEA), which was truly a great tool that has now served its purpose. The auto industry has wrung out the maximum benefit from the approach and needs a new driving force in order to achieve the next level.

The auto industry—in fact, all industry—needs to make sure the actions of engineering and management guarantee operator success. Here's an example: quality of products is typically measured in the parts per million (PPM) that are defective. Most suppliers in the auto industry perform at 200 PPM or better, which means their performance is 99.98% good and 0.02% defective (2 bad products out of 10,000).

The operator followed an exact and perfect set of steps almost all the time, but 2 times out of 10,000 tries, the operator did the process differently and made an unacceptable part. This chapter highlights the deficiencies of FMEA and compares the strategy to the concept of error-proofing, known in this book as Success Every Time (SET).

SET uses simple error-proofing devices that guide each operator's efforts to help him *not* do things differently those two times. Each part is made exactly right; if it isn't, you stop the process and start over. This concept differs, however, from mistake-proofing. In this chapter, the two terms are also defined.

A Brief FMEA Overview

If you are familiar with FMEA, skip this section and head to the "SET as an Alternative" section a bit later in this chapter. But in case you are not familiar with it, FMEA is a method to systematically look for everything that can go wrong and to look for ways to address it. It's a combination of lessons learned (what went wrong in the past and how those issues were resolved) and a variation on Murphy's Law by looking for everything that could go wrong and taking steps to address them. It is based on a logical method that ranks the risks and helps manufacturers focus time and energy on the area that can cause the greatest problems and, therefore, greatest costs.

FMEA's Three Elements of Risk

At the heart of the FMEA approach is risk prioritization and it is based on three very smart elements of risk all differentiated on a scale of 1 to 10:

■ **Severity:** How badly can the problem affect a customer? Problems that can harm people get the highest risk ratings. Issues that are mere inconveniences have successively lower ratings.
■ **Occurrence rating:** How often does the problem happen? Issues that happen once in million times are obviously rare (low risk). Problems that happen every day need more focus and get the higher score.
■ **Detection capability:** How likely are we to spot the defect and then protect the customer? If the problem is easy to identify and spotted all the time, it's a low risk. If only the customer can catch it, you maximize the risk of dissatisfaction.

This approach is so logical and direct; it is difficult to argue with it. In fact, the greatest asset of the FMEA is that it can be applied to various levels of design and manufacturing. At the design level, you can look for common problems and install simple remedies. For example, in your car, there are mechanical features in the steering column that won't let you remove the keys unless the shifter is in the park position. This helps to prevent your car from rolling down a hill; the design forces you to shift the car into park before you can remove your keys.

You can use the FMEA method to look for problems at the processing level, too. When you are pumping gas into your car and the pump senses some back pressure, the pump shuts off. Sometimes it's due to the tank being full and the shutdown is ideal to prevent spilling gas. On other occasions, you may not have placed the nozzle properly and the flow of gasoline hit the side wall of the filler tube. The shutoff stops the process and notifies you to take the necessary actions. The failure mode is the possible spilling of gas, and the FMEA approach did a great job of finding some very logical problems and creating a smart solution to some common problems. In this arena, the FMEA process is great and works well.

This tool has been effective in bringing the industry a long way in improving quality. The problem is, the FMEA approach cannot cost effectively take the industry to the next level. This was best articulated in the Spring of 2007 when prominent quality manager Robert Naski said, "FMEAs are a great starting point; however, the number of failure possibilities are endless. The FMEAs have taken us a long way but we need something different."

FMEA's Three Major Limitations

FMEA has three major limitations; they are described in the following sections.

Bias Toward High Severity

In the FMEA method, the three factors of Severity, Occurrence, and Detection are combined to create a risk prioritization. To do this, each factor is given a score from 1 to 10, and the three numbers are multiplied together to generate a Risk Priority Number. This is a relatively simple and straightforward method that's meant to identify and prioritize the risks and help drive people to mitigate the effects. The difficulty with most problems is people can figure out ways to reduce the frequency of a problem happening (Occurrence improvements) and they can also come up with ways to find defects better (Detection), but there is no way to reduce the impact to the customer. The Severity factor is relatively fixed, and engineers can do little to change it. They can improve the other two factors (and they do), but they have only rare opportunities to improve the Severity rating.

When people focus their energy on the high-risk operations, they will have a built-in bias to focus on the problems that have the greatest risk of harm. Although this is the right activity to take, the reality of the world is that we have already managed these high, harm-related risks extremely well.

Today's competitive world has driven most of these items to a very negligible level. (I know there still are risks and watching for the most severe problems absolutely needs to be retained, but the issues are nowhere near the volume or severity that existed twenty-five years ago when the FMEA method started in the automotive industry.)

The majority of problems seen in manufacturing today are now mostly aggravations. They rarely are the types of shortcomings that harm. Most customer complaints come from parts or features that don't operate to expectation. When you look at independent customer surveys, people describe their complaints with descriptions like "The car doesn't heat up fast enough in the winter," or "the radio reception is too scratchy." It used to be the "heater doesn't work" or the "tape deck ate up my cassette." See the shift? This is happening all the time. The problems customers are complaining about are much less harmful to people or property, and yet the volume of different issues is growing. This is because the past focus of FMEA has worked. We have taken care of the high-severity issues fairly well, and we are operating at an extremely high state of control on these high-severity matters.

Ever-Increasing Opportunity

As engineers work beyond the high-severity issues, they walk into a problem of scope. The high-severity items are the *critical few*. There are a handful of products and processes that carry the most risk exposure. At the same time, there are thousands of parts and processes that represent the *trivial many.* In practice, the world of automotive manufacturing has matured to a situation where companies that manage the trivial many, the best are the ones that win. FMEAs no longer provide an effective filter to know where to apply resources. Today, all issues are equally important regardless of the severity: Anything can disappoint the customer and the cars are so good, the winners are the ones with the *relative quality differences*—those tiny improvements that make one car company look better than the next. This widespread quality improvement trend means each company must focus every single operation it has in order to prosper. Every operation is an opportunity to make or break the company's reputation in the eyes of its customers.

The Infinite Volume of Possible Problems

When conducting an FMEA, engineers will sit down and review every step in making a part, list all the possible failures for each operation, and then write down a step to control the possibility. The problem is, the possibilities for failure are infinite. A failure can be as common as a knife blade becoming dull due to normal use or as infrequent as an ice storm in Hawaii. When focusing on FMEA as a means to remain competitive, the practical problem is that you are essentially chasing infinity. This is hugely wasteful, frustrating, and limiting in terms of the return on the hours invested. I was in a conversation with Kim Fleming, a well-respected automotive quality professional, and we discussed the shortcoming of FMEAs as follows:

FMEAs are like a 12-foot ladder. As you discover a new concern, identifying the problem and coming up with a solution are like adding a layer of tape to the top rung enabling you to reach a little higher. If you keep adding more layers of tape, essentially you are making the 12-foot ladder taller and taller but in a slow and laborious way. The shortcoming is that we have to climb 20 feet. If we keep adding layers of tape, we will get there eventually. What we really need is an extension for the ladder instead of applying more tape faster.

The difference between the FMEA approach and the SET approach can best be described in a Ying Yang diagram as illustrated in Figure 1.1. In the world of manufacturing, every operation performs work and can either be done right or done wrong. In the FMEA approach, you focus on stopping activities in the "done wrong" side. But as time goes on, we discover new problems we never thought of and find new ways to do it wrong. The list of possibilities grows and grows and the time, effort, and expense to protect us from this list grow in proportion.

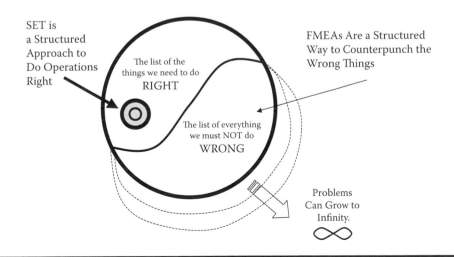

Figure 1.1   A view of manufacturing planning.

This continued pursuit of infinity may be a solid explanation of why, after twenty-five years, the auto industry still has trouble creating totally comprehensive FMEAs to catch every problem. Anyone facing an infinite task like this will look for shortcuts, take risks, or just go as far as time and energy permit and stop, which is exactly what has happened to the FMEA process. It has passed the point of diminished returns. We need something different now.

SET as the Alternative

With SET, by concentrating on the elements that drive success, you focus on a much smaller set of actions than the infinite listing of what can go wrong (as is the case with FMEA). You define what *must go right* and set up error-proofing devices on these actions to help operators do their work exactly right.

Errors occur on the line because disruptions distract operators from doing their jobs in the usual way. A distraction may last a few seconds or a few minutes, but as soon as an operator has a small mental lapse, a mistake may be made. Although distractions are normal and entirely human, they still cause errors.

SET invests in error-proofing devices to help operators remember what to do, and help them do it right. One operator I worked with described it this way, "Set the system up so that the process is telling me everything I need to know." For operators, it is just as easy to make a part correctly as it is to make a part improperly, so you generally won't get any resistance about the SET approach, as long as the error-proofing devices are easy to use.

The Difference Between Error-Proofing and Mistake-Proofing (and a Little About Poke-Yoke)

You may be thinking that SET is simply a different way of describing the poke-yoke processes used all over Japan. (*Poke-yoke* is defined as devices that help operators notice common human mistakes.) But SET is much larger. Here's why: most quality systems look for a means of detecting defects, many of which are discovered one at a time. In the automotive industry, you see this all the time: find a problem and react by installing a poke-yoke. *Poke-Yoke* by Shimbon is an excellent book to identify, create, and invent devices that can help you spot defects. It is a great starting point. The problem with systems that only detect defects—rather than prevent them—is that they place you in reactionary mode.

In this section, I clarify the terminology of poke-yoke, error-proofing, and mistake-proofing. Poke-yokes are devices that notice differences that a human might miss and the difference can cause a defect. If you place a poke-yoke device into a station in such a manner that the operator cannot start the value-adding action unless everything is correct, you have prevented the creation of the bad part. Poke-yoke devices that *prevent bad product creation* are defined as error-proofing devices.

However, not all poke-yoke devices prevent bad product creation. You can also install poke-yoke devices to perform a part inspection action to check for defects after the part has received its value-add. In this situation, if a bad part has been created due to an operator mistake, the poke-yoke device identifies the part as possessing the mistake and points it out to people in order to protect your customer.

Succinctly, error-proofing devices prevent defective parts from existing, while mistake-proofing devices identify defective parts that exist. Both use poke-yoke devices, but the placement and intent differ. It's poke-yoke's effect on the value-added portion of the process that distinguishes error-proofing (in which no bad part exists) from mistake-proofing.

SET is a method that helps people maximize the profit-creating potential of poke-yoke devices through strategic placement and integration into your operations. It has two key pieces.

- **Sensing device:** The first feature of error-proofing is the use of some type of mechanism or sensing device that assures that, at this workstation, everything is exactly right.
- **Control element:** The second feature is a control element that will allow the operation to proceed only if the device senses that every element is right. If every element is not right, the defective operation is stopped before the actual error is built in to the product.

Either the product is right or it is stopped. Effective use of error-proofing is the ideal state because it prevents defects from being created in the first place.

Mistake-proofing, on the other hand, is the next best approach. This is a system designed to determine what happens *after* an error has occurred, identifying mistakes that have already occurred and stops the process so the defect cannot be passed along. It does not, however, stop the defect from occurring in the first place. Instead, the defect or mistake exists, the mistake-proofing device spots it, stops the process from adding any more value on a known defect, and alerts operators to take action. Mistake-proofing is always less effective than error-proofing because operators have to deal with correcting or disposing of the substandard part and this correcting or disposing is not always done correctly. If bad parts regularly exist in your system, you are at risk.

Understanding Mistake-Proofing Devices

A device that can identify a defect that has already occurred is called a *mistake-proofing device.* A bad part has been started, the mistake exists, mistake-proofing devices find the problems, and the devices prevent the continuation of the condition—most importantly to keep it out of the hands of the customers. A mistake-proofing device, then, is detection-centered, spotting problems that have already occurred and making them obvious to people for special handling. The handling options of bad parts are straightforward: either fix the problem or properly dispose of the bad parts. The key is to have the mistake-detection device as close to the point of origin as possible, the closer to the point of cause, the less chance of adding any additional value being to the product. There are four distinct types of mistake-proofing devices.

- **Detection within the station of manufacture.** Letting people know a mistake has been made before moving to the next point. For example, double typing of computer passwords and the way cars won't let you remove the keys from the ignition unless the shifter is placed in "Park."
- **Mistake detection built into the design of the components that makes the mistake obvious.** Packaging on toy kits with markings for the exact number of screws and nuts is one example. If one is left over, you probably forgot to install one of them. Other examples include outline drawings on tool benches showing storage locations and color coding of mating components to aid in assembly, making sure the right parts are assembled with their partners.
- **Mistake detection within the workstation.** Examples include chimes in your car when you open the door or your keys are left in the ignition; a light and buzzer if you don't latch your seat belt. For both of these "errors," you get a signal that you're not in an ideal condition, but you have the power to proceed despite the warning.
- **Mistake detection in a downstream operation or subsequent operation.** For example, a chime in your car when the door is partially open and spell-check that is imposed on users automatically before they save a document or send an e-mail. Both error-proofing and mistake-proofing

have a common element, however, which is they both are processes that are built-in to work on 100% of the parts and are deployed 100% of the time. They are always working on every single unit.

There Is a Place for Mistake-Proofing

There are many times when a cost-effective error-proofing device is not possible to absolutely prevent the problem, so spotting the problem through mistake-proofing is the next best thing.

An automatic teller machine (ATM) provides a great example. If you make a mistake and type in the wrong personal identification number, the ATM stops the process and makes you correct it. You made the mistake, but the machine caught it at the point of occurrence (or in production terminology, at the point of manufacture). Likewise, if you are making a withdrawal and you type in an unusual number, the ATM notices the mistake and stops the process for correction. The machine also will not give you more cash than is in your account.

Contrasting Mistake-Proofing Devices and Error-Proofing Devices

To understand the key differences between error- and mistake-proofing devices, you need to understand that all devices fall neatly into a two categories—the type of control they exert and the point at which recognition of the error occurs.

- **Type of control:** Devices can either *prevent* an error or *detect* a mistake. *Prevent* means the defect is stopped before the value-add cycle can begin, so no bad part even exists. *Detect* means the defective part exists but the production process identifies it so people can cull it from the production stream.
- **Point of recognition:** The point upon which the recognition occurs falls into three categories:
  - It is built into the physical design of the product
  - It is built into the point of manufacture or human use of the tools
  - It is built into a subsequent point *after* the mistake has been made

The matrix in Figure 1.2 plots out the type of control along with the point of recognition. Error-proofing is limited to two very specific cells, in the "prevent" column, in the physical design, and at the point of human interaction.

You encounter thousands of error-proofing devices in everyday life. Here's a simple one: when you use your automatic teller machine card for a cash withdrawal, you must punch in a dollar amount in increments of $10. This is

	Prevention	Detection
In the Component Design	**IDEAL** 1. The design forces the parts to go together only one way, the right way. Error cannot be made	**STRONG** 4. The design creates an obvious highlighting feature when a mistake is made. Error easily identified
At the Point of Manufacture	**EXTREMELY STRONG** 2. The tools, fixtures, and other devices have features that point out the mistake and stop the operator from making the part. Error creation is stopped	**STRONG** 5. The tools, fixtures, and other devices have features that find the mistake and alert people to take immediate action. Error identified immediately
In a Subsequent Operation	**VERY GOOD** 3. A process is built into an operation to check previous work done. If a previous error occurred, the total component cannot be completed until corrections can be made. Final operation is stopped	**GOOD** 6. An inspection device is part of a subsequent operation. It highlights a previous error and alerts the person at the subsequent operation. Isolates the customer 100%

☐ = Mistake proof   ▨ = Error proof

Figure 1.2 Error- and mistake-proofing positioning.

because the machine has only $10 and $20 bills. It is forcing a match between what you type in and what cash the machine can dispense. It is built-in—you cannot make an error and type in requests with any other denomination. For cash disbursements, it is error-proofed for cash in units of $10.

Russell Williams, an operations director at Mark IV Automotive, made a great observation about a student in a class of his:

> I saw Zo (a lady in the class) pick up a coffee cup, bump it on a book, and spill a small amount on the table. I know Zo, she is a dedicated, smart person, fully capable of picking up that cup of coffee and raising it over the book. She didn't intend to spill the coffee, it just was an inadvertent mistake by a good person. It just happened, just as small things just happen by smart dedicated people in the production floor. They need better tools put in place to help them execute the right process, every time. Let me repeat the heart of the message: They need better tools to help them execute the right process, every time.

Recognizing True Error-Proofing Devices

Consider the following examples of true error-proofing devices:

- Prevention devices are built into the physical part design (square peg and round hole), such as electrical connectors with different designs and shapes forcing one-way assembly, and prepackaged coffee for in-room hotel coffeemakers.
- Prevention devices are built into the point of manufacture, like an automatic teller machine that will not let you insert the debit card unless the magnetic strip is in the right orientation, credit card readers looking for inactive and over-the-limit accounts, bill accepters for soft drink machines that check for counterfeit money, and computer password security modules preventing unauthorized people from accessing my files.

The six-panel matrix in Figure 1.2 illustrates the categories of error- and mistake-proofing and how they fit together in a logical pattern, based on the "prevent" and "detect" concepts.

You will notice in the matrix a number in the upper right-hand corner of each cell. This number identifies the relative power of each approach. The only true error-proofing elements are the tools that are in cells 1 and 2 (prevention in either the design or in the initial station). These are best because they stop the process before any value is added to the product. If you can eliminate the possibility for a bad part to exist, you cannot have a defective part. Either you make great products or you don't produce; it's either good or it doesn't exist.

That's SET in a nutshell: determine a way to protect the customers on each and every operation in the plant by installing devices that work on every single part to detect whether anything is wrong, with simplicity as the key.

Recognizing Features of the Best Error-Proofing Devices

That's obviously an ambitious objective. Words like "every" and "anything" are all encompassing. Many people only see higher costs and overkill. If you approach it the wrong way, error-proofing can be hugely expensive and complex. This is not what I am suggesting. You want to keep SET as simple as possible and install the devices with a bias toward those that are inexpensive and lower risk.

Therefore, the best error-proofing devices:

- Work constantly.
- Are built into the natural flow of the operators.

- Are very simple and inexpensive.
- Need only natural properties in order to work (for example, gravity).
- In addition, you want to utilize such devices in areas where the cost is easy to justify:
  - Any moderately risky task that follows a high value-add (in other words, you don't want to allow a high value, good part to become bad at a subsequent low value-add operation)
  - A job that tends to gets buried in the component and must be right in order for your part to properly function
  - Job set-up activities that can be error-proofed and minimize the creation of batches of substandard parts
  - Error-proofing placed on critical process controls to keep them operating as designed

Focusing Error-Proofing Devices on Three Specific Areas

When doing a job or making a part, there are three specific areas where the error-proofing needs to be focused.

- Value-added actions, such as the work of operators in their daily assembly and manufacturing tasks.
- Job set-up elements, such as getting the right tools and fixtures lined up the right way, having the correct set of component parts, and making sure tooling is properly tuned and maintained.
- Processing parameters—that is, critical settings that must be in place to do the job right. Temperatures, pressures, speeds, feed rates, and so on are the parameters that govern success and are predictable and definable.

In strategic error-proofing, a complete set of devices would include devices to hold all the variables in these three categories within proper control and force people to do things the correct way, placing a bias on simplicity. Note that these three areas (value-added actions, job set-up elements, and processing parameters) are the subject of Chapters 4, 5, and 6, respectively.

The key to error-proofing is preventative action; that is, you cannot get started making the mistake without encountering a process to make sure you do it right. There is a significant premium on error-proofing devices because they stop waste before it occurs. If you can't create the defect, you have not invested any value into the product and you cannot proceed any further. If there is no product, there cannot be any mistake, and you cannot continue to pour good money after bad because the bad money was never spent.

There is an additional benefit to error-proofing devices over mistake-proofing devices: there is no need for any handling of the waste or the substandard products. Follow the process and make only products that are right—nothing is simpler. This makes error-proofing the best counterpunch to all the cost of low quality.

A Quick Look At Sophisticated High-Tech Devices

In many situations, the simple physical interference type error-proofing is just not possible. You have to move into more advanced solutions like proximity sensors and limit switches. What's more, a lot of engineers will be enticed to move into the very high-tech solutions like computerized vision systems.

Although the capability of high-tech devices is exciting, the complexity creates some disadvantages when it goes onto the floor for production. Complex items are typically full of a lot of individual components, and if one component fails, the unit goes down, which not only removes the error-proofing device from the system and leaves the system vulnerable, but also opens the temptation for people to tamper with the device. This is particularly relevant with software.

Key Points

- The world of manufacturing products falls into two categories:
  - Actions that are right
  - Actions that are wrong
- Failure Modes and Effects Analysis (FMEA) is a useful tool that:
  - Focuses on what can go wrong
  - Has a structured method to reduce the risk of these things that can go wrong
  - Calls for structured analysis process
  - Has an infinite number of conditions that can go wrong
- Poke-yokes are devices that can sense differences or mistakes. The placement of the poke-yoke classifies the device into two categories:
  - An error-proofing poke-yoke prevents a bad part from being made
  - A mistake-proofing poke-yoke detects a bad part after it has been made and alerts operators to act in order to protect customers
- SET is a stronger tool than FMEA or mistake-proofing that:
  - Focuses on the set of activities that needs to go right

- Motivates the creation of tools to help people follow only the exact right steps
- Has a greater capacity than FMEA because it proactively prevents problems and is easier to perform because there is a finite group of actions to control

■ SET can simultaneously:
- Lower your costs of scrap and rework
- Increase your first-time yield and productivity
- Improve your warranty performance
- Increase your profits

Chapter 2

Success Every Time and Quality Improvement

Ask yourself this simple question: What justifies paying a premium for products and services—a Lexus or BMW, a wool suit, an expensive haircut? More often than not, the answer is related to the *quality* of the product.

In the auto industry, when you mention Lexus, Mercedes, or BMW, you immediately think of high price, high performance, and high quality. But in the case of Cadillac, which used to be the high-quality name of the auto industry, the mistakes of the 1970s through the 1990s soiled the company's reputation so badly that most people consider it a tainted player in this league. The company had a period during which the product did not live up to the image, and the trust between General Motors and its customers was lost. The resentment and bitterness of poor quality has remained for decades and may last the lifetime of the people affected. Cadillac is fighting back, and I hope it makes it, but I wonder how many customers the company lost for life to other brands.

Why Quality Matters (Hint: Profits!)

As a producer of goods or services, what do you get if you have quality products? Your answer will always trail its way to the bottom line: profits. What is so perplexing and absolutely astonishing, though, is that when you talk to business leaders, they often don't see this link between quality and profits.

When you are producing quality products, you are making each one right, every time. When you make products right, you have less (or no) scrap and rework, which means lower costs. Lower costs yield greater profits. When you make products right, the plant runs with a higher yield and allows you to make more products on the same equipment and with the same number of people, and this, too, means more profits. When you make products right, your customers are happy and have fewer complaints, which means fewer warranty claims, which again lowers your costs and gets you more profits. When you make products the right way, you communicate to your customers that you can be trusted, and they will pay a premium for your goods or services, which means more revenue at a lower cost, which means more profit.

Why don't business leaders get this? I hear all about cost cutting, plant consolidations, and layoffs and mergers, all with an eye toward improving profits. Yet these cuts almost always fail to produce higher profits. Why? Because quality suffers, customers get lost in the process, and they end up walking away. Without customers (or with ticked-off customers), you are going to lose. It is absolutely astonishing that CEOs and upper management spend so much time on schedules, costs, budgets, and matters of money without spending at least as much time on quality and on driving the enablers to achieve quality in their products. Quality is the only multi-leverage point. When you improve quality, you get more profit, more sales, higher asset utilization, more customer loyalty, and the right to charge a higher price. The SET method is designed to simultaneously maximize your top line revenue and bottom-line profits.

SET helps you significantly improve your profits by helping operators do the right things, notice their mistakes the moment they occur, and properly address those errors before problems can escape. This method has zero operating costs, functions 100% of the time, and gives you 100% successes every time. Any way you cut that equation, it is good. The caveat is that not every production situation allows for SET, especially those with a high degree of craftsmanship like manually painted products or custom fitted parts like seat covers on chairs, but when combined with other strategic moves (see Chapter 10), profits can still go up.

The SET process is the answer to one of the more perplexing problems of management: "why do we always seem to have time to fix things but we never have time to prevent them in the first place?" I believe that is the wrong question. I think the question really is, "why do we have a number of systematic methods that helps us fix errors, but we don't have a logical approach to help us prevent them in the first place?" That question is the crux of the SET method.

In the words of Mark Wrobbel, a respected quality professional in the auto industry,

> We need something in this auto industry that puts quality in a positive light. Everything we do is based on avoiding some type of negative. We need a method to focus on the elements necessary to make a product good instead of looking at the infinite number of things that can go wrong. We need something to drive us toward what needs to go right.

SET is that driver.

Getting Suppliers SET

It is important to realize that the SET method needs to extend to your suppliers. Your customers want your finished products to be perfect, which means the subcomponent parts that you buy from your suppliers need to be perfect as well. SET needs to be done across your entire supply chain because the quality of your purchased parts is just as important to your customers as the work done in your factory.

Quality in the Automotive Industry: A Quick Primer

In the automotive industry, the importance of the supply chain is huge. Most original equipment manufacturers (OEMs; like Ford, GM, and Chrysler) purchase more than 70% of their components, and the trend is for increased purchased content, especially for the traditional Big Three U.S. automakers. But parts from suppliers must be right because the expectation in the market is for zero defects and the supply chain must deliver in order to get there. There is no tolerance for defects.

So if a supplier has a difficult time shipping parts to specification (spec), the industry does two strange things. The first thing we do is to insist on inspection, getting some people to look more closely at the parts and see whether they can spot the problems and place them aside. The idea is that even if you have to double or triple the inspection, you protect the supply chain from defects.

If that doesn't work, inspection companies are available for hire, so the automakers force the production supplier to go out and hire a company to inspect the parts the supplier has made. Inspection on top of inspection, all in the interest of protecting the customer; but it results in huge costs and huge wastes, all in the interest of quality.

There are three perspectives on this that need to be explained.

■ From the automaker's perspective, they are paying for good parts and deserve the protection provided by this redundant inspection. The automaker's job is to assemble perfect vehicles, so parts must be made to spec. If the automaker has to replace parts, either in warranty or in the assembly plant, they incur the expense and reduce their profits. This can justify their action to insist on the inspection activity deployment.

■ From an accountability point of view, one theory holds that the low bid supplier was awarded the job, and forcing them to produce to spec— even if it's through inspection—is a means to "teach them a lesson." If you take a risk and deploy an inferior process, you should have to encounter the cost of poor quality and make sure on the next bid that a more reliable process is used.

■ Finally, a lot of people believe that the best way to get management's attention is through the supplier's pocketbook. Having the supplier pay for someone else to check their work is not only insulting but also runs up a significant financial burden that must be dealt with in order to remain profitable. Margins in the auto industry are tight. These unanticipated costs, especially the cost of nonquality, can destroy plant viability and livelihoods of families, in addition to the corporate balance sheets and income statements. What could be a greater motivator than survival? Threaten a company's survival and you will get their focus, or so the theory goes.

Although the total sale of automobiles is a huge figure, it is a finite amount. You can pick your favorite company—Toyota, General Motors, Ford, Volkswagen—and if they sell a unit for $20,000, they retain $6,000 to cover their costs of production, development, and everything else, leaving $14,000 to distribute to their 3,000 suppliers. That's only a little over $4 per part for all the supplier costs. In this industry, the margins are razor thin. Once you start driving up the costs of daily operations, you deplete the lifeblood for the future. There is no avenue for price increases. The market has so many alternatives that price increases almost always results in the loss of business.

The reality of this world is that redundant inspection is rampant. But it doesn't work because you cannot inspect in quality. And the bottom line is more and more waste. Manufacturing experts believe over $500 million is spent annually in the auto industry working to protect customers from defects using redundant third-party inspection alone. This is a huge investment in trying to protect their reputation.

Waste erodes profits, which is death to a company. Profits attract the best management. Profits provide the resources to invest in new products and new technology. Profits make the supply chain stronger and make the competitive position of the manufacturer and the suppliers better in the market. Profits allow the supply chain to maintain or improve their manufacturing processes.

Reducing the profits does the opposite. They start the death spiral of less maintenance of the equipment, making the process more vulnerable to problems and scrap. If you have to scrap more, you have to run more in order to meet volume needs, making less time available for maintenance, tooling, and training, and resulting in even greater losses.

Two Basic Kinds of Quality Problems: Predictable Ones and Surprises

There are two kinds of quality problems, ones that are "predictable" and ones that are complete surprises. With complete surprises, there is nothing much you can do. The September 11 attacks, for example, were a complete surprise. Nobody predicted what was going to occur, and we were totally vulnerable. Unexpected, unpredictable total surprises are very hard to prepare for and prevent. Fortunately, they also are quite rare. Although we don't welcome these things, it is hard to go much past reasonable protection to guard against them.

On the other hand, there are a huge set of problems that fall into the category of likely and predictable. When you fill your car with gas, it's very predictable that people will forget to re-install the gas cap. Years ago, gas stations would have boxes full of caps that people just forgot. Today, this has been error-proofed. On almost all cars, the gas cap has a plastic strap attaching the cap to the car. You cannot make the error of leaving the cap at the gas station; it stays with the car and flip-flops on the side of the car until you notice it later. This simple device works 100% of the time. It's a smart and inexpensive solution to a known problem.

This type of thinking and approach is the mind-set that must permeate the entire manufacturing industry. Most quality problems *are* predictable. They have happened in the past; we know what they are and where our routine vulnerability is.

The Quality Implications of the Production Method Used by Every Operator at Every Company

Every day, production people make perfect parts and when they do, they always follow the same steps:

- They select the exact part(s) needed and place the part(s).
- They use tools and fixtures to properly orient and align the part(s).
- They perform a value-adding function to the part(s).

All operators follow these three steps, everywhere products are made, and always with varying levels of success.

SET is a strategy that drives companies to deploy error-proofing devices that govern these three steps. You want to help operators follow the exact process and if anything is not exactly right, you want the process stopped for corrections. These three steps are the dominant factors for quality.

When you look at these steps, it can be quite easy to define the correct activities, and then to take the initiative to find very simple and 100% effective methods to help the operator go through the cycle. Essentially, they need to make sure they select the right part, position and orient it correctly, and apply the right value-added function. The SET method ensures they make these three steps in an error-free way.

The Set Method: Part Level, Set-up Level, and Parameter Level

The SET method involves three major levels:

- **Part level:** The first step is to look at the part itself. All parts have a distinguishing characteristic that makes them different from all the other parts in the world. When the person selects the part, you need to use the unique characteristic of the part to make sure the operator has taken the correct one. With some simple preplanning, all parts should have a few unique identifiers that can facilitate physical contact to help people use the right parts.

■ **Set-up level:** The second piece of the puzzle is to help the operators who perform the task of changing production from one part number to the next as they set up the various jobs. Because the set-up process affects every part in the new batch, this activity is critical to your success and can be broken down into a small set of various discrete items:
  – Materials: The right parts are in each production cell
  – Tools and fixtures: Correct items, appropriate for production
  – Alignment and settings: How the fixtures and equipment are adjusted

■ **Parameter level:** The final aspect is the way in which the force that helps the parts change state is induced on each individual part. Manufactured items typically change state when energy is applied to the part for a set period of time. If you are cooking, you apply heat as energy for a time period. If you are cutting wood, you are applying a cutting friction force as the energy. Whatever the job is, the parameters for error-proofing to know you have done the job correctly are:
  – Energy or force applied
  – Time

These three basics levels of SET—the building blocks, if you will—are very discrete. At every workstation you have actions by operators who select parts, place them in a precise location, and add some type of value to them. This means you need to have the correct parts available, make sure the correct tools are available and that fixtures are aligned the right way during the job set-up activity, and ensure that equipment devotes the correct value-added energy to the parts as measured by the correct parameters. The model in Figure 2.1 Basic Success Elements places these three factors as sides of a pyramid.

Within each of these sides of the pyramid are a discrete set of actions that are easy to define and monitor. Chapter 3 gives you an overview of these actions, while Chapters 4, 5, and 6 specifically cover the part, set-up, and parameter levels, respectively.

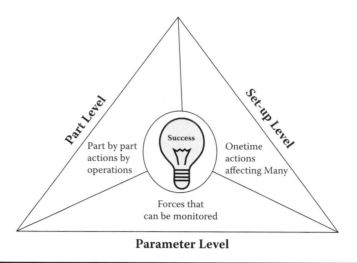

Figure 2.1   Basic success elements.

Key Points

- Quality is such a necessity that businesses are willing to incur huge costs to protect customers and the company's reputation. Some companies invest in double and triple inspection, which is extremely costly.
- Helping production operators with devices that allow only the ideal process to occur is a smarter method than adding levels of inspection.
- The best choice is to recognize that problems fall into two obvious categories:
  - Predictable: The issues where you want to focus proactively
  - Unpredictable: The issues that can only be addressed reactively
- The SET method addresses the predictable category of problems.
- The three levels of the SET method that govern every manufacturing process are the part level, the set-up level, and the parameter level.

THE CRITICAL PHASES OF SUCCESS EVERY TIME

Chapter 3

Strategic Monitoring of the Critical Elements

The entire focus of Success Every Time (SET) is to concentrate the talent of the engineers for them to deploy devices that help operators make each part perfectly. For any operation, operators (1) select and handle the parts they need, (2) use tools and fixtures to properly orient and align the parts, and (3) use some force to add value to the part. You need a process that focuses on these three critical elements, provides devices that guide operators' actions, and helps them to do only the correct steps. You then need to monitor each manufactured unit at the part level, the set-up level, and the parameter level.

Part Level: Monitoring Each Unit of Production

The first phase of monitoring with SET is monitoring the components for each individual unit of production. Every time a production cycle occurs, you are making one unit. The production operator selects a set of parts and places them into one or more fixtures to manufacture or assemble one unit. The devices at the part level are intended to track the precision of the placement of each component part that goes into each unit made. Chapter 4 discusses part-level monitoring in detail.

Set-up Level: Monitoring the Initial Set Up

The second level of monitoring is to verify that the job set-up activity is correct. Once the set-up tooling action is complete for a specific operation, the individual parts, tools, and the equipment work together while that batch is being run.

For most production operations, companies use fixed tooling and equipment to make many different parts. A stamping press is specifically designed to have internal dies changed so that it can be used for many different activities. The same concept goes for injection molding presses, spot welders, and other universal machines that are designed to provide specific value-added energy in many different ways. They are cost effective because of their interchangeability.

The set-up activity is very important. The set up controls the proper positioning of the individual parts and lines up the necessary tools. The key variables in the set-up phase are (1) having the correct set of tools in place, and (2) aligning the tools properly. The method that confirms these two steps have been done correctly is the monitoring of the process at the set-up level. See Chapter 5 for additional details.

Parameter Level: Monitoring Equipment Inputs

In any manufacturing company, the concept of a value-adding activity needs little explanation. However, I define *value-add* as an action that changes the state of a product through the imposition of some type of energy. If you take a sheet of steel and insert it into a stamping press, you change the state of the steel because of the force of the press. The value is added to the steel because you imposed the force of the press on the steel. Similarly, if you take a tire and mount it on a rim, you have changed the state of the tire and rim into a more functional assembly by stretching the internal bead of the tire over the rim. Here, the base concept is the value-adding energy.

In SET, the point of value-add has two critical elements. The first, make sure everything to select and position the parts is correct because after you add the value, you have created either success or failure (and you only want success).

The second is the monitoring of the energy parameters to provide the right amount. Imagine a plastic injection-molding machine. The part to have value-added is usually some type of thermoplastic, and the press has a mold or die that is set internally in the press. You know you need a discrete amount of plastic, usually measured by weight (parameter 1). You also need the plastic at a proper temperature (parameter 2). With the proper amount of heated plastic in place, you need the press to inject the liquid plastic into the mold with a specific amount of force (parameter 3) applied over a specific amount of time (parameter 4). Once the plastic has been injected to the mold, the plastic needs time to cool and return to a solid state that can be measured by cooling time (parameter 5) as well as mold temperature (parameter 6).

In this example, there are six monitored parameters that can help you achieve success every time. If the production cycle has all six parameters exactly right, you make a great part (provided the correct plastic—the correct part—has been chosen and the set up is correct). Chapter 6 shares details about parameter-level monitoring.

Turning the Engineer Loose

With SET, your engineer has a road map he or she can follow to become a proactive problem solver versus a reactive one. Being proactive, your engineers are preventing problems in the world of human interface at the workstation level. There are many levels of problems in production: nonrobust designs, incapable processes, lack of disciplined maintenance, and so on.

Count on your engineers and let them be creative; most will establish highly effective solutions to error-proof your processes. They will find switches that have a universal function that they can apply to hundreds of their cells at a fraction of the cost and speed, while also being simple to maintain. They will be able to strategically place these devices before the value-adding process and prevent scrap. They will be able to help your people see and control the parts that have a high likelihood of warranty issues and keep these parts out of the hands of your customers. Your productivity will go up, your quality will go up, your customer satisfaction will go up, and your profits will go up, all by deploying this strategic method. Better ideas will pop up as time goes on, and with the SET method, they will be able to see the opportunities to deploy the better methods with minimal effort.

Two Examples: Making Chocolate Chip Cookies and Mounting Tires

Most people have made chocolate chip cookies, which is a fun process that offers a great payoff. When a master baker makes them, they come out perfect every time. When I make them, they are pretty good but there is a definite difference between mine and professional ones. A master baker has a defined set of actions that I can't quite duplicate.

Here is the approach of a master: start by taking out the butter and letting it sit in the bowl to warm up (part level: butter; parameter level: softness defined by temperature and time; set-up level: oven temperature and placement of the proper mixing bowl on the counter). When this baker gets ready to get into the mixing, he turns on the oven (set-up level: oven preheat) and goes through each operation step-by-step, increasing the value of the batter as he goes. Step one is to mix the butter, sugar, and vanilla until creamy (part level: correct ingredients; parameter level: amount of each ingredient, mixing method, time, and creaminess). I can follow this same sequence.

Step two is to mix in the eggs. The method is in phases, so the baker adds in one egg at a time, mixing thoroughly for a better blended consistency. To duplicate this method, I would benefit by having a small two-egg holder (set-up level: devices to confirm the correct materials, the eggs) that releases one egg at a time and requires me to dispose of the shell after picking up the first egg (part level: sequence control) and not allowing me to start mixing until the shell is in the garbage can. Simultaneously, the sequence would not let me get the second egg until the batter had been mixed for the proper amount of time (parameter level: mixing time and number of spoon strokes). This basic cycle repeats as I progress into the flour-adding phase, then into the chocolate-chip-adding phase, and then into the scoop-it-onto-the-baking-tray phase. Last, you head into the baking process (parameter level: time, temperature, humidity) before going into the cooling-and-removing-from-the-cookie-sheet phase.

For each step, there is an identifiable process that contains parameters. If you can set up a method with extremely simple and effective reminder mechanisms to define those parameters and help people stay within those parameters, you would achieve success every time.

If I wanted to make this a simple method to follow, I could tape a note around two sticks of butter in the refrigerator that says, "Open these and place them in the green bowl and place them on the counter," thus allowing time for the butter to soften during the next step. Next, the instructions would say to get into the car and buy a dozen eggs and fresh chocolate chips, and do not take another step until all twelve eggs are properly placed into the storage bin in the refrigerator. In the egg bin there would be another note: "Open the oven door and get more directions." Inside the oven is a note: "Turn on the oven to 350 degrees," along with a symbol for each ingredient. Show a cup of brown sugar, a cup of granulated sugar, two teaspoons with the word *vanilla*. And so on. This concept is illustrated in Figure 3.1.

Now you may be thinking that this sounds like operator instructions. Define the list of steps one by one and have the person do it. In one way, it is. These are the steps for success. In reality, however, it is more. This error-proofed strategy is providing devices to help the operator follow the steps, with welcomed reminders and controls to help him or her do the steps successfully every time. The steps are made on ongoing reminders that make the process impossible to do wrong. It is these up-front steps, reminders, and devices that are needed in industry.

In the world of business, we are not making homemade cookies. We are making sophisticated products and doing so in an extremely competitive environment, with cost controls and excellent efficiency rates. We have to deal with multiple shifts, employee turnover, and different kinds of complexity. Although the fun of making cookies in a treasure hunt fashion would not work in business, the thought pattern of defining exactly what is needed in each step and providing simple, effective controls and reminders will tremendously increase your chance for success and help where it matters most: with each and every part you make and place it into the hands of your customers.

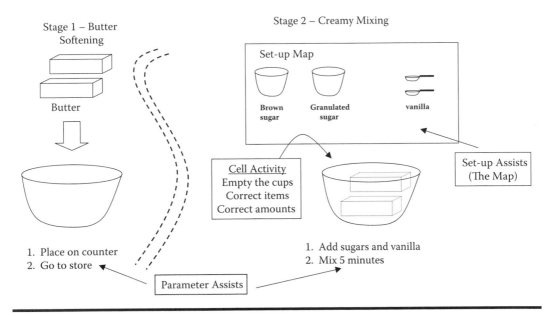

Figure 3.1 Making chocolate chip cookies.

Let's take another example, mounting a car tire onto a rim. When you go to a tire store, the action of the mechanic to mount the tire is a repeatable task that can be explained with the SET process. Begin at the starting point, at which a wheel rim is placed on the tire-and-rim assembly machine.

■ The first action is that the mechanic selects the rim (part level: part selection activity) and places it on the center spindle (part level: rim orientation and precise part placement).

■ The next action is to secure the rim to the fixture using a locking ring to prevent the rim from jumping off the fixture in the later step when the tire is stretched into place (part level: proper selection and placement of the locking ring).

■ Next the tire is positioned over the rim (part level: selection and placement) followed by the attachment of the tire bead stretching tool between the tire and rim (part level: selection and proper placement).

The mechanic is now at the point of value-add, the force to stretch the tire bead attaching it to the rim. If the previous steps have been done correctly, the tire bead pops over the rim, and he has added value to the product. The tire assembly machine had to be set up properly with the fixtures to hold the rim square to the center spindle as well as having the correct bead stretching arm and rim locking ring (set-up level: alignment and proper tools available). The tire-and-rim assembly machine needed to have the correct amount of torque in the center spindle to provide the stretching power for the tire bead and the spindle needs to spin 360 degrees around the rim in order to complete the cycle (parameter level: torque and spindle rotational angles completed).

The concept of SET focuses on the process of production and has the basic monitoring elements included. It applies to any manufacturing cycle as diverse as making cookies or putting car tires on rims. The fundamental steps are universal!

Key Points

■ To achieve success every time, you need to focus on the critical few elements that define success.

■ The focal points of SET are:
  – Actions by operators to select and place *parts*

  – Precision of the job *set-up* of the right tools and the right alignment
  – *Parameters* of the value-adding energy imposed on the parts
■ The SET process will motivate the best identification and positioning of an error-proofing monitoring device that will help operators always perform each job with the correct set of actions.

Chapter 4

Phase I of the Success Every Time Method: Part Level

The first phase of SET involves looking at every individual part at every workstation, making sure each is the correct part, properly oriented, and placed in the exact ideal location. This phase of the SET method helps operators on the few times they do the process incorrectly, providing simple error-proofing devices that notice something is incorrect.

The SET method is a step-by-step process that guides thinking patterns, so engineers and managers can help their operators in a different way. What is the key in this approach is the strategic position; people with a desire to help can randomly error-proof. They can come up with and install devices that are directionally correct but do not knit together as a best approach that considers multiple dimensions. For example, you may define a great car as one that has excellent fuel economy, looks beautiful, has a significant level of features, and is reliable. Given those multiple factors, how do you choose the one that's most important to you?

The same complexity of multiple dimensions exists on great error-proofing devices. How can you systematically, in a step-by-step manner, understand the trade-offs and evaluate the optimal device based on your situation? This chapter helps you do just that.

I start the analysis at the part level. Here are the steps that are illustrated in Figure 4.1:

1. List all the operations required to make a particular product.
2. List the activities performed at each operation that must go right.

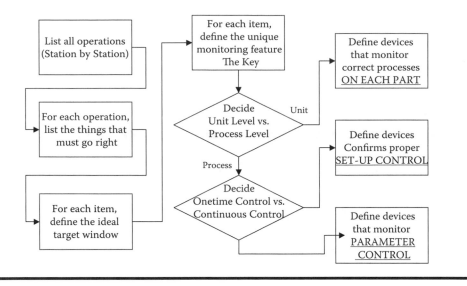

Figure 4.1 SET method logic.

3. Define the ideal target(s) for each activity.
4. Detail the key identifying feature(s) on each part.
5. Identify an error-proofing device for each activity.
6. Rate the effectiveness of the device.

Step 1: List the Operations Required to Make a Particular Product

To start the SET process, the first step is to make a list of the activities that the product encounters as it goes through the process to receive its value. These are the logical work activities that are typically done at the individual workstation level. You're going to answer the question: What does the production worker do? The answer may be identical to the operator's work instruction for the workstation. Everything else is based on this foundation element, so you need to define the exact actions that make a great product.

As you proceed, let's follow the example started in Chapter 3, the activity to mount a car tire on a rim.

The list of operations to mount the tire on the rim is as follows:

1. Place the rim on the tire and rim machine.
2. Place the tire on the tire and rim machine.

3. Press the inner tire bead over the rim.
4. Press the outer tire bead over the rim.
5. Inflate the tire.
6. Balance the assembly.
7. Install the tire and wheel assembly onto the car.

Step 2: List the Activities Performed at Each Operation

Next, you need to list the activities performed in each station to make the part correctly. This is the list of activities that needs to be followed, always in the same set of actions, in order to succeed. The basic steps are as follows:

- Select the exact part(s) needed and place the part(s).
- Use tools and fixtures to properly orient and align the part(s).
- Perform a value-adding function to the part(s).

Using the first few operations of the tire-and-rim mounting example, the activities of the operations are as follows:

Operation 1: Place the rim on the tire and rim machine

- Select: Obtain one rim specified by the customer.
- Orient: Place the rim over the spindle with the decorative side facing up.
- Orient: Rotate the rim on the machine with the tire valve on the right.
- Place: The rim center hole must make 360-degree contact with the spindle.
- Place: The rim must be horizontal.
- Value-add: Screw down the locking ring securing the rim to the machine.

Operation 2: Place the tire on the tire and rim machine

- Select: Obtain one tire specified by the customer.
- Orient: Place the tire over the rim with decorative side (raised or white letters, etc.) facing up.
- Place: Locate the tire at an angle to match the tire positioning fixture making contact at points A and B of the fixture.
- Value-add: None in this step.

Operation 3: Press the inner tire bead over the rim

- Select: Obtain the bead stretching arm.
- Orient: Orient the arm with the slotted end away from the tire.
- Orient: Orient the arm with the tire stretching tracking bar up.
- Place: Hook the tire stretching end between the tire and rim touching both rim and tire simultaneously.
- Place: Place the slotted end over matching tab on spindle.
- Place: Have the slotted end of the stretching bar contact base of drive spindle.

All you are doing in this step is defining the standard work for the operator that shows how a great part is created. This is the work instruction for the operators with some very specific elements on select, orient, and placement of the individual components.

Step 3: Define the Ideal Target for Each Activity

For each activity performed at the workstation, you need to define the ideal target with enough precision that can be used by the error-proofing device as the specification to be monitored and assured.

The Ideal Action and Target

For every specific task, there is an ideal action that can produce the best result with the minimal effort. In the Toyota Production System, this concept is at the heart of standardized work. Find the best method you can, do it over and over the same way, and get the same (excellent) result. Take the example of professional basketball players, especially those who are great free throw shooters (and there aren't many). If you watch the great ones, they have a strict routine that they follow religiously. The Detroit Pistons' Richard Hamilton is a good example of this. When he shoots a free throw, he stands in an exact spot, with his body positioned in an exact way. When he gets the ball from the referee, he bounces the ball twice in front of him and once to his right side, and then he sets himself with the ball in an exact manner and shoots it in a timed cadence. He probably does it hundreds of times a day, the same way, to get the ideal action. His target is making the basket, but he also has in mind a flight pattern for the ball, a particular swishing sound when the ball hits the net, and a particular sway of the net itself when the ball goes through it. It's all very precise in terms of his target.

For success every time, you need the set of actions and targets for every individual workstation and every action at that workstation. You can provide physical examples of the targets and use them throughout the plant. You can provide tools and devices to help operators perform the tasks they are doing over and over again. The basketball environment does not fit with these types of devices because the court is not dedicated to one person shooting free throws. In the manufacturing workplace, however, you do not have this same need for universality, so you can set up devices to help you significantly increase your odds of success.

If you are going to monitor actions within each workstation, you need to specify your standard of "good." Consider the example of the tire and rim mounting for operation 1:

■ Select: Obtain one rim specified by the customer.
■ Ideal target: Part number on rim matches customer order.
■ Orient: Place the rim over the spindle with the decorative side facing up.
■ Ideal target: Decorative side up.
■ Orient: Rotate the rim on the machine with the tire valve on the right.
■ Ideal target: Tire valve located between 80 and 100 degrees (about the 3:00 position), using top, dead center as away from tire holding fixture.
■ Place: The rim center hole must make 360-degree contact with the spindle.
■ Ideal target: Visible contact at all points.
■ Place: The rim must be horizontal.
■ Ideal target: Plus or minus 2 degrees to horizontal.
■ Value-add: Screw down the locking ring securing the rim to the machine.
■ Ideal target: Torque of 10 Newton-meters.

As you look at each element, you are defining the monitoring points with a degree of clarity to be able to differentiate "good." You are looking for enough specific information to help us seek devices that quickly and inexpensively sense when the operation should be allowed to proceed.

Step 4: Detail the Key Identifying Feature on the Part

The key identifying feature of the part is the unique element on the component part that will be used to help us determine good from anything else. (Chapter 7 has more information on providing key identifying features on your parts.) This feature is used as the reference point for the error-proofing device that monitors and governs the action at the workstation. This key is the critical reference point for the parts and the error-proofing device(s).

If you find that many parts do not have these reference points, you may have a huge realization. In the words of Jim Lenhardt, an operations manager with multiplant responsibilities, "this can be a huge 'ah-hah moment.' If you have no absolute reference point, you are vulnerable, pure and simple."

You may occasionally find that no reference point is plausible, especially in batch processing where you do not have specific features to monitor on the individual components, and we will need to look for other means to drive success. An example of this is the production of fluid-type product, such as wine. The winemaker can look at the grapes going into the process, but he cannot distinguish the individual grapes that go into the specific bottle you may purchase at the store. If the winemaker wants to make you happy, he has to control the entire batch of grapes because they are intertwined in the winemaking process. Monitoring the specific product that the individual customer receives is not feasible in batch processing. In such cases, you will need to define your set-up and operating parameters extremely well. On the other hand, you may encounter situations where a unique reference point is possible but, for whatever reason, none exists. When this happens you have a choice: either build a reference point into the part design or continue in the vulnerable condition and intensify the set-up and parameter controls.

Step 5: Identify an Error-Proofing Device for Each Activity

For each activity at the workstation, identify an error-proofing device that can assist operators in performing the action in exactly the correct fashion relative to the targets. The error-proofing device needs to help guide the operation into the correct actions each and every time and drive an appropriate action when the exact correct action is not taken. The device has to be capable of either (1) confirming the right action and let the part proceed or (2) forcing the system to confront the condition immediately and completely.

This sounds simple, but finding devices that effectively meet a number of different needs requires a lot of thinking and imagination and hard work. The best devices satisfy a number of criteria simultaneously. They are highly effective, cost conscious, friendly to all operators, fast, add no extra work, *and* have 100% uptime. Finding devices that meet all these criteria is a tough challenge, yet with practice and experience these devices become obvious and available to you. What you need is a systematic means to drive your thinking to find devices that satisfy as many of these criteria as possible.

Step 6: Rate the Effectiveness of the Device

If you rate the effectiveness of the device in a logical pattern, you can determine where you are most secure. This rating activity is multidimensional. One day while looking for a model to illustrate the concept, I came up with the pyramid shown in Figure 4.2 to show the concept of a great error-proofing device with different levels of interaction.

All error-proofing devices are not created equal, so all of them need to be analyzed against the multiple aspects demanded for success. When looking at individual devices, you'll find different levels of utility, but effective error-proofing can go far beyond the device itself. When strategically viewed, devices can assist in other productivity arenas, helping with one-piece flow and acting as monitors for the proper sequence of operation.

When you look at error-proofing strategically, you can design devices to create multiple benefits for you, instead of solely detecting good versus other. To enjoy this larger set of benefits, you need a method or a system

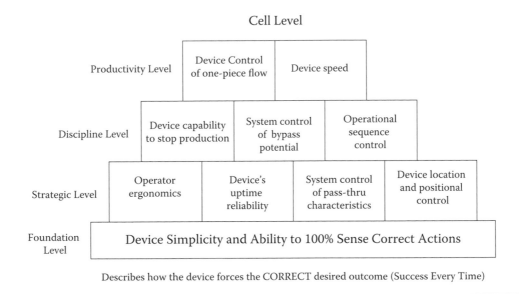

Figure 4.2   SET device rating pyramid.

that encourages your company to be more creative. Many people stop short of designing for this larger set of benefits because there is no reason to look deeper. You need a system that drives the right actions, encouraging this additional creativity.

I see the key dimensions to evaluation devices as a pyramid with a foundation and different levels of advantages. In the device rating pyramid in Figure 4.2, the layers are discussed in the following sections.

Foundation Level (Simplicity and Permanence)

This level looks at the overall simplicity of the device as well as its overall permanence of operation. The best devices are in effect 100% of the time, have low initial cost, no ongoing costs, and are simple to operate and maintain.

For example, a fixture with pins identifies a necessary hole in a part works all the time. If the hole is not present, the pin has a physical interference, and the part can't go into the fixture. This device works every time, has a low initial cost, has no ongoing costs, is simple, and is 100% reliable.

The least desirable devices are complicated, high-tech options. Although technology is great, highly complex devices require a significant amount of technical skill—as well as money—to maintain. When they break down they often take a long time to repair. I have seen many of these devices work well, and they do some things that simpler devices cannot do, so there is a place for them. But for the most part, they are less preferable to the more simple devices that work all the time.

Strategic Level (Protection)

At this level, you are looking for the device to protect you from some common vulnerabilities.

- How well do operators like the devices and enjoy having them around? If they don't like the device, they will be motivated to defeat it. If they like the device, they will welcome it at their workstation.
- Will the device keep working all the time? Is the uptime good? The best devices from an uptime perspective seem to be simple, for example, the pins that fit into the holes on the part. The least effective are highly complex vision systems that require specially trained technicians to maintain.

- Can the device check the parts that your company buys from your suppliers and make sure you don't pass through a defect from your supplier to your customer? The customer doesn't really care where the defect originated, they know they purchased the item from your company, and your reputation is soiled due to a mistake from your supplier.
- Are the devices placed properly? On a strategic level, where you place your devices is critical. Ideally, you want only perfect products in the hands of your customers, and you want to eliminate scrap at the same time. In this ideal world, you have error-proofing devices that can stop any value-adding step (activities that change the state of the part) if the fundamental elements are not right. In the perfect world, monitors would allow the operators to complete their cycle only if everything were right in the first place. Unfortunately, this ideal world is not always possible. If you can't have the ideal world, what is the next-best option? You want to place the devices in the best spot possible to either stop the creation of a bad part or, if an error is made, it must be at a point where you can detect and remove the bad part out of the value stream as early as possible.

The Last Station

In any production operation, there is a last station. This "position" in the line is always critical because any mistake made by your last operator can be found only by your customer because, by definition, you have no one behind your last operator, as shown in Figure 4.3. The control of this last position on the line (positional control) can mean the difference between error-free products for customers and customers who are dissatisfied. (The term *positional control* is used to illustrate the need for a stronger degree of control of your success on the last

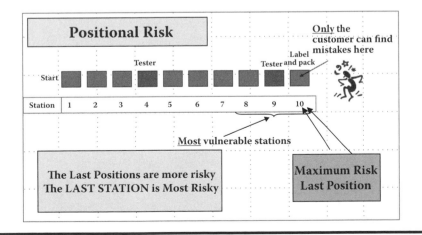

Figure 4.3   Positional control.

operations.) Recognize that all operators can make mistakes, yet your reputation is most vulnerable to mistakes made by your operators at the end of the line. Your best strategy for protection is to have the strongest degree of control possible in the last few stations.

Discipline Level (When Defects Are Found)

When devices are intelligently integrated into the system of production, your operation can protect the customer by forcing an action when a defect is found. The entire foundation of SET is to make sure the part is right or it's not sent to the customer. Integrating the sensing ability of the device with the forced action that you want is the ultimate method to assure control. On the first level, if the device finds something outside of the target, you want the process to stop. If the operator can address the condition and get it right, you want to start again and finish making the part. It is a definite advantage to drive this type of thinking into your process because it saves you money and complaints.

In the discipline level is the concept of bypass control. Bypass is a situation in which an operator skips a production step. He or she has a part in hand, gets distracted in some way, and inadvertently moves an unfinished part to the next operation. The part bypassed a station. Integrating simple counting devices can sense that a 25th part has come into a station but the previous station has only processed 24. The device can be set to stop the 25th part and send it back for processing. Such a device can't always prevent the bypass from occurring, but it can stop the further processing and help you can avoid this waste.

Another aspect of discipline is the proper sequencing of steps. When baking chocolate chip cookies, if you dump all the ingredients in the bowl right at the start, you can end up with a giant mess. The batter will get clumpy because the flour absorbs the moisture of the eggs too fast, or you have to mix the batter too long and you end up smashing the chocolate chips. On the other hand, if you follow the ideal sequence the consistency and quality go up.

In an assembly operation, threaded fasteners, specifically nuts and bolts, are used on products to hold parts together. There are times when the order of fastening each nut or screw can control the final quality of your product. Let me provide an example that is illustrated in Figure 4.4.

The radio in your car has four corners, and there are screws behind the surface that fasten the radio to the instrument panel. The ideal pattern to tighten the screws begins at the top left followed in a crisscross pattern that

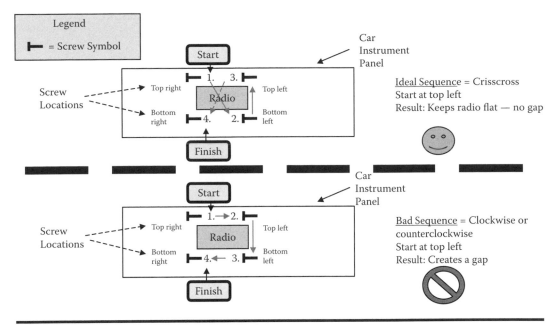

Figure 4.4   Effect of operational sequence control.

secures the bottom right screw second, the top right third, and the bottom left last. This crisscross pattern does a great job of keeping the radio flat to the instrument panel and keeps the operator from creating gaps. If the operator follows a clockwise or counterclockwise pattern, the fastening sequence will pull the first edge closer to the instrument panel and create a gap on the opposite side. The quality of the product in this case is affected by the sequence of actions that the operator takes. If the sequence of the operation is important to your product's success, devices can be programmed to help people follow your desired order and reduce your variation.

Productivity Level

At the production level, a few last factors involve increasing your total throughput, and they can help you increase both quality and profits. In manufacturing, you want to be as efficient as possible, letting operators produce as fast as they can safely, so speed is a factor. The second factor is the overall synchronization between operations, with all operators proceeding at approximately the same pace. The productivity level of success every time aims to find devices that help you produce as quickly as possible while simultaneously keeping the overall operation in control.

Regarding speed, some devices work immediately or can perform their functions faster than a human. These are the ideal. On the other hand, some devices require a little time and impose nuisance delays for the operator. The worst are the ones that slow the operator down; these are the ones where the operator will find a method to defeat the device. While the tolerance for delays is really determined by the individual person, a good rule of thumb is if the device imposes more that a 5% time burden on the operator, he or she will find a way around it. For example, if a normal cycle is sixty seconds, if the device takes less than three seconds to detect and act, most operators will tolerate the delay. More than three seconds, and they will become frustrated. The ideal situation is to have the device be faster that the cycle so no burden is present. Error-proofing devices must not slow the rate of production in any way.

Regarding synchronization and balance, many people believe the Toyota Production System (TPS) is the most efficient production method. Over the past decade, many companies have worked to implement synchronous manufacturing operations, in which all the people in a cell produce parts simultaneously. The one-piece flow approach, one of the foundations of the TPS, can be integrated into many error-proofing devices quite easily. For example, in most of today's production systems, inexpensive switches are used to start or stop production equipment, sense proper activity in a cell, and monitor one-piece flow. This is a foundation of the TPS. One piece flow means that all workers have the responsibility to complete their jobs and when they are done, they hand their finished pieces to the very next person. Nobody can start the next cycle until everyone along the line is finished. Everyone works on one piece at a time. Operators are prevented from building up inventory between stations; only one piece at a time is allowed. The TPS is easily enabled and monitored by devices and can help people eliminate waste and gain productivity.

The Part Level Device Rating Matrix

Great devices possess a combination of all of these features and can be rated by how well they combine these features. Think of a great basketball player like Michael Jordan, who was great because he had multiple talents. He was fast. He was competitive and willing to practice harder than most. He was willing to share success with his teammates. He was a great shooter when the pressure was on.

Level		Criteria	Score
Foundation Level		**1. Simplicity and Ability**	
	Ideal	Constant — uses laws of nature	4
	Robust	Simple — uses low-tech shelf items	2
	Capable	Complicated — needs technical support	1
Strategic Level		**2. Operator Ergonomics**	
	Ideal	Ambidextrous/unisex (RH/LH male/female)	4
	Robust	Welcomed by operators	2
		3. Devices Uptime & Reliability	
	Ideal	Works all the time without maintenance	4
	Robust	Downtime less than 10 minutes per quarter	2
	Capable	Downtime less than 10 minutes per month	1
		4. Control of Pass Thru	
	Robust	Confirms all critical features from Tier 2	2
	Capable	Confirms customer attachment points	1
		5. Positional	
	Ideal	Error-proof is done before the cycle can start	4
	Robust	Confirms success in the station	2
	Capable	Confirmation is done in the subsequent station	1
	Max Risk	Last station (multiply total score by)	.66
	Risk	Two stations before last (multiply total by)	.85

Level		Criteria	Score
Discipline Level		**6. Stop Production**	
	Ideal	Operation stopped for correction or immediate marking of defect and immediate containment into a controlled condition	4
	Capable	Operation stopped for human intervention	1
		7. By-pass control	
	Robust	Part must pass thru station AND confirmed in subsequent station	2
	Capable	Confirmation is downstream	1
		8. Operational Sequence Control (When Needed)	
	Robust	Sequence sensitive actions are device controlled	2
	Capable	Sequence sensitive actions are device monitored	1
	Ignored	Sequence sensitive actions are human dependen	–1
Productivity Level		**9. One-Piece Flow**	
	Robust	Devices tied between stations. Previous station is stopped until subsequent station is started	2
	Capable	Devices tied between stations with controlled buffers	1
		10. Device Speed	
	Robust	Devices do not slow cycle time	2
	Capable	Devices slow cycle time less than 5%	1

Figure 4.5 Part level device rating matrix.

The same goes for great devices and to determine how well they operate on a number of levels, you can rate them systemically. Take a look at Figure 4.5, which gives you a numbering system for each of the elements described in this chapter. When you look at each criterion, the individual number identifies the relative power your device has for that element. The overall strength of the device at the part level is the sum of the individual scores for each category. Just add them up.

A Few Words on Arbitrary, Threshold, and Minimum Scoring Ideas

When instituting a device rating system, you may be tempted to use the numbering system to drive some type of minimum rating standard. My experience has shown that having minimums drives very bad behaviors. Having thresholds or minimums encourages evaluators to:

- Overstate the true capability of the device.
- Engage in minimalist thinking (creative laziness due to hitting a number).
- Create waste because some rating categories are irrelevant to certain stations.

A rating system is a great way to know whether the device is offering the support to the operator that you need it to and also helps you see where the device's relative strengths and weaknesses lie. The matrix is aimed at driving success and driving the right actions.

The SET Summary Form

As you move thorough the SET method, you will begin to accumulate your knowledge into a form (see Figure 4.6) that creates a strategic advantage for you.

Use this form to capture relevant information on the error-proofing devices you use to help operators select and place each part. In Chapters 5 and 6, you will build in additional information as you discuss the elements in the set-up and parameter levels.

Success Likelihood Number

The ultimate outcome, after completing the sections discussed in Chapters 5 and 6, is to create a picture of how strong you have made each individual operation. You are seeking operator success, so the final outcome of all of this work is the creation of a Success Likelihood Number. The *Success Likelihood Number* is a score for each individual operation that combines the level of support you have built into your processes.

Operation	Part Level					Set-up Level		Parameter Level			P O S	Success Likelihood Number
	Key Feature	Ideal Action	Target	Device	Part Level Score	Method	Set-up Level Score	Parameter Target Amount	Method	Part Level Score		
											1	
											1	
											1	
											1	
											1	
											1	
											1	
											1	
											1	
											1	
											.85	
											.85	
											.66	

Figure 4.6   The Success Every Time (SET) summary form.

> *Note:* The SET scoring system is similar to the approach used in the FMEA process discussed in Chapter 1, where the risk of an operation is described in a Risk Priority Number that combines the failure mode's severity, detection, and occurrence scores.
>
> In the SET method, you will be combining the strength of the devices you have chosen and multiplying the scores from the part level, set-up level, and parameter level.

Take a look at the SET summary form (see Figure 4.6) in some detail. The first column provides a space to list each operation. Columns 2 through 4 ask for the key features, the operators' ideal actions, and the target part placement that you have defined while going through this chapter. In Column 5, a space is provided to describe the specific device you plan to deploy to help each operator's part placement hit the described target. When this is completed, analyze your chosen device and add up the point values from the device rating matrix (see Figure 4.4) that best describes the features for your device. In Column 6 a place is provided to insert your part level score.

After you have read and completed Chapters 5 and 6, you will end up with a measure that reflects the relative strength of your error-proofing devices at the operator level, beginning with the part level and extending to the set-up (see Chapter 5) and parameter (see Chapter 6) levels.

The culmination of these factors will determine the overall success likelihood of each operation. As you will see in Chapter 6, the Success Likelihood Number will be determined by multiplying the scores of the part level, the set-up level, and the parameter level scores.

Key Points

- Establishing great devices at the part level is a logical step-by-step process:
  - List all the operations required to make a particular product
  - List the activities performed at each operation that must go right
  - Define the ideal target(s) for each activity
  - Detail the key identifying feature(s) on each part
  - Identify an error-proofing device for each activity
  - Rate the effectiveness of the device
- Drive your thinking to create key identifying features on each part that will be used to confirm operators are being successful.

- Identify and rate each device in a systematic manner:
  - Foundation level: The ability to detect 100% the simplicity of the device
  - Strategic level: The appeal of the devices to people and business with factors of operator friendliness, uptime, bypass, and positional control
  - Discipline level: Integrate the devices to enhance disciplined execution
  - Productivity level: Find fast devices that encourage one-piece flow
- Place the relevant information on the SET summary form.
- Avoid using thresholds. The best way is to recognize relative strength and risk and use the knowledge to drive continuous improvement.

Chapter 5

Phase II of the Success Every Time Method: Set-up Level

Each workstation in a production setting has actions that can be monitored to an individual unit you sell to your customers, although you also have actions that are not always traceable to that unit. The set of elements in the set-up activity of the tools are not always traceable to each individual part sold, yet they are equally critical because of the direct impact they have on that sellable unit. This chapter describes a method to help you recognize and monitor the most relevant activities that need to be controlled at the set-up level.

Figure 5.1 highlights the activities of the set-up level, in which skilled job setters gather all the tools and materials and align the tools with the equipment in order to do the job. The set-up actions typically govern the entire batch of production, which means the set-up activities have a leveraging influence: a mistake during set-up can affect a large quantity of parts.

If you wanted to duplicate an ideal action, you would need to look at the basic success elements. Breaking these elements down into pieces, you have activities at the part and station levels and activities at the process level. The process level has two main activities (set-up actions), which do not tend to vary much during processing, along with activities that have variation requiring monitoring.

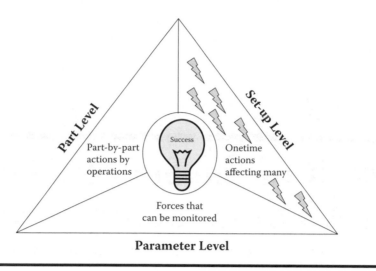

Figure 5.1   Basic success elements set-up level.

Understanding Why Job Set-up Level Is So Critical

In all of production, job set-up may be the most critical to a production organization's success, yet many companies spend only a cursory amount of time focusing on it.

When a job set-up is done right, you move from one part to another relatively quickly, with minimal disruption. Dave Hartz, a quality systems trainer and team leader, described it this way:

The great companies focus on this job set-up like the pit crew of a racing team, in order to gain a competitive edge. You have to do it right. You have to do it fast. Make a mistake, and you're headed toward some losses.

Unfortunately, I have seen multimillion-dollar recalls from an undetected mistake during the set-up of some process. It happens to every automaker and probably to every manufacturer of any type of goods. As a consumer who watches the news, you hear about these recalls because they are at the retail customer's end. But plenty more situations occur in which the retail customer is protected, but profits were still lost. Within the manufacturing chain of any product, manufacturers find batches of materials that they place on hold and either scrap out or return. This is pure waste.

With great losses on the line, you might think manufacturers would focus on this step with intense focus, but most don't focus hard enough. Why? We in the auto industry typically have our most experienced, conscientious, intelligent, and trustworthy operators doing the set-up. We tend to trust them because of these attributes. At the same time, however, these operators are people just like you and me, and they make mistakes like the rest of us. I like the phrase used by Kurt Vogler, a quality assurance and audit expert: "What we don't do enough of is to make it easy for people to succeed. It seems we have a habit of making it hard on them."

Generic Actions for a Typical Job Set-up Event

In nearly every manufacturing facility, when production processes are changed to stop making one specific part and start producing a different one, skilled set-up people do the following:

1. Purge the line of the previous parts (Raw, Defects, Finished, etc.).
2. Document any known problems with tools or fixtures.
3. Capture the last part as a reference point for the next start up.
4. Remove the tools and fixtures from the former job (store and repair as needed).
5. Deliver and position the correct parts for the next job.
6. Confirm that repairs to tools and fixtures were conducted properly.
7. Install the needed tools and fixtures in the correct locations.
8. Set all operating parameters to the designated levels for each station.
9. Produce a controlled set of parts to test the new line set.
10. Check the new parts off the new set-up standard.
11. Release the job to the operator(s).

This is a lot of activity, and it sees a significant amount of variation, time, and pressure. If you have a production operation with a lot of stations, you have eleven discrete elements going on for each station, all of which must go right. Most of the time, the job set-up activity can be performed only when the production line is stopped. This results in a loss of production, and, therefore, a loss of profits. Of course, this means that management wants the set-up done quickly and perfectly.

Error-Proofing the Job Set up

If you work in manufacturing, look at the various methods for job set up in your facility and describe what you see. What is remarkable is that well over 65% of manufacturing operations use the two least reliable methods to confirm job set-ups (relying on the memories of job set-up operators and relying on written checklists) because their job set-up people have been around so long and know their job requirements very well.

Using Job Set up Verification Methods

The two biggest mistakes when setting up a job are relying on memory and using a written checklist as "verification" that it was done properly. In the first case, the job set-up operator just "knows" that the set up was done correctly. This may or may not be true, but it is the method often relied on. As for the written checklist, you will hear terms like *tool sheets, set-up sheets,* and others, but it all boils down to some type of list. Ask yourself, would a car racing team rely on written instructions or checklists, all performed by one person, without rigorous verification? I doubt it.

Notice in Figure 5.2 a set-up confirmation method diagram, a grey dotted line in the center of the list. Almost all the items below the line are totally dependent on the set-up person not making a mistake. If he or she misses something, a percentage of production is likely to build 100% of the batch in a substandard manner until the defect is noticed. In Figure 5.2, a double verified checklist is also included in the substandard confirmation group because operators, both the job setter and the person verifying, don't have enough time to read during the pressure of setting up the next job. They will end up doing a superficial job, glossing over details, and assuming all is

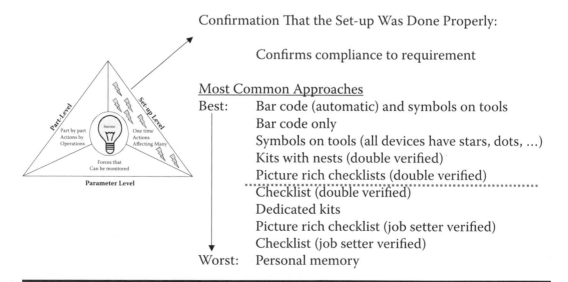

Figure 5.2   Job set-up confirmation methods.

well. In the words of a colleague of mine, Jim Hare, "You need to watch out for the lists; people will have a tendency to pencil whip it."

So what can you do instead? First, don't rely on checklists or memories. Instead, you need your engineers to design devices and other job set-up verification methods that make sure set-ups are performed correctly every time. What you need are verification methods that help set-up operators know which method is correct and confirm its proper execution.

Look at all the steps of a typical job set up (in the "Generic Actions for a Typical Job Set-Up Event" section) and give yourself a score on how well you confirm each set-up operation (i.e., each distinct set up) using the rating system shown in Figure 5.3. As much as possible, go for the highest score you can get with the money you have available.

One such example is to create tool kits with nests, which simply means that tools are nested together in a logical way—all tools that are used to manufacture a particular unit, for example, are grouped together, each with its own obvious place so that none is omitted or replaced with a different tool. If you take the time to create tool kits with nests, most job setters will love them because it makes their jobs easier (in fact, many have created such tool kit nests on their own over the years). This is a great first step. But you still need a verification process, like combining a kit/nest with color-coding symbols for verification. With such a method, you are creating verification, so that all the eyes of the team are looking at the set-up. However, the "looking over the shoulder aspect" is so subtle that the set-up operators don't necessarily realize that a double check is in effect. If all the tools on the line used to manufacture a particular unit have a blue X on them, for example, and after a job set-up to make that unit one tool on the line has a black circle instead, the operator knows something is not right, and this mistake is easily spotted and corrected before problems in the manufacturing process occur. This is a simple, low-cost, highly effective,

Method	Score
Barcode (automatic) with symbols on tools	10
Bar code only	8
Kits with nests and symbols on tools	8
Symbols on tools (all devices have stars, dots, ...)	6
Kits with nests (double verified)	5
Picture rich checklists (double verified)	3
Checklist (double verified)	1

Figure 5.3　Job set-up rating matrix.

redundant verification process that works constantly with minimal maintenance. All job setters need something like this.

Employing SMEDD

While a full explanation is not within the scope of this book, consider the business practices described in a single minute exchange of dies and devices (SMEDD). *SMEDD* is a structured approach to make the changeover process as efficient as possible. The approach looks at die changes as a process with discrete steps, and it defines ways to minimize the waste of changing over a line. It starts with maintenance of tools, which is performed between production runs, and also with the proper storage of tool sets. The next step is scheduling and staging, in which operators line up everything needed for the job set up and stage all elements before the changeover takes place. This staging activity usually employs the kits with nests, so it's easy to confirm that you have everything you need ready to go (all the tools, all the parts, all the gauges, and so on). There is a place for everything.

The SET Summary Form

When the changeover happens, there are places (kits) for all the retiring tools and parts, making it simple to get everything obsolete out of the cell to make room for everything going in. In the SET job set-up scoring system in Figure 5.4, this concept is rewarded with one of the highest scores possible.

You will need to build on the work performed in Chapter 4 by adding the set-up level information to the SET summary form. In Column 7, list the type of set-up method you plan to put into place, and in Column 8, list the score from Figure 5.3. You will continue using this form in Chapter 6.

After you read and complete Chapter 6, you will end with a measure that reflects the relative strength of your error-proofing devices at the operator level, beginning with the part level (Chapter 4), extending to the set-up level, and then including the parameter level (Chapter 6).

The culmination of these factors will determine the overall success likelihood of each operation. As you will see in Chapter 6, the Success Likelihood Number will be determined by multiplying the scores of the part level, the set-up level, and the parameter-level scores.

Operation	Part Level					Set-up Level		Parameter Level						Success Likelihood Number
	Key Feature	Ideal Action	Target	Device	Part Level Score	Method	Set-up Level Score	Parameter Target Amount	Method	Part Level Score	P	O	S	
													1	
													1	
													1	
													1	
													1	
													1	
													1	
													1	
													1	
													1	
													.85	
													.85	
													.66	
						Column 7	Column 8							

Figure 5.4 The SET summary form.

Key Points

- Most companies have come to rely on the least effective methods of set-up verification, which are the set-up operators' memories and written checklists.
- Better, inexpensive methods of verification are possible with a small amount of planning.
- Set-up monitoring is best performed when all of the people in the manufacturing process have easy means to confirm that the right tools are in place and aligned in the proper fashion.
- To best gauge the error-proofing nature of your job set-ups, insert the appropriate score in the summary form as the set-up metric that will be used in the calculation of the Success Likelihood Number.

Chapter 6

Phase III of the Success Every Time Method: Parameter Level

The parameter level is the last segment of the SET method: identifying devices that can confirm that the value-added action on the part is operating in the ideal window for the situation. Take a look at Figure 6.1: the base of the SET pyramid is the parameter level, which is the true value that your company adds to its products. Always keep in mind that your customers are paying you to do this value-adding step perfectly.

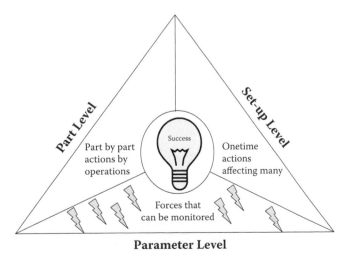

Figure 6.1   Basic success elements: parameter level.

Understanding Value-Added Energy

Value-added energy changes the part in some way. If you are securing a bracket with a bolt, the value-added energy is the torque on the bolt. It is important to illustrate that there are times when multiple parameters are needed to be monitored in order to have complete information. In the example of torque on a bolt, monitoring only the torque load can be incomplete. Consider the possibility that the threads on the bolt were damaged in some way. You could achieve the specified torque but the joint would not be secure because the bolt was only run halfway down when the damaged thread was encountered and the torque load was attained. The torque can be measured in a number of ways; most commonly it's measured as actual torque but as this example explains you may need to monitor multiple parameters such as the number of turns of the screw (commonly measured in angles of rotation). If you are soldering electrical components on a printed circuit board, the value-added energy is a measurable element of heat applied to the solder for some period of time. You need the properly tightened screws to secure the parts together and you need the solder to hold the components on the printed circuit board adding the value of allowing the electricity to flow. Both of these are examples of the value-added energy measurable as an operating parameter that is traceable to each part.

Remember the tire to rim mounting example I discussed in Chapter 4? There are a few parameters in that example that make sense to monitor.

- The first parameter is the torque force on the central spindle that rotates around the rim and stretches the tire bead over the rim.
- The second parameter is to monitor the spindle's 360-degree rotation to make sure it goes all the way around the wheel.
- Next, the mechanic needs to inflate the tire so air pressure could be an intelligent parameter.
- Finally, once the tire is installed, the balancing operation could get monitored by watching items like the speed of the spinning tire.

In each of these examples, SET is looking to confirm that the proper energy to complete the value-add was present and induced on the individual part that is headed for your customer.

Reviewing Common Forms That Parameters May Take

Parameters usually take one or more of the following forms:

- Concentricity.
- Current.
- Feed rate.
- Humidity.
- Pressure.
- Purity.
- Resistance.
- Specific gravity.
- Speed.
- Surface tension.
- Temperature.
- Time.
- Torque.
- Viscosity.
- Voltage.
- Volume.

Although this is not an exhaustive list, it is interesting how few true parameters need continual monitoring. It is very likely that your operation deals extensively with somewhere between six and twelve base parameters, matching the unique features of each specific part design. You need to become outstanding at monitoring this small set of the critical few, and do it constantly and in small enough segments that you can apply reasonable batch control that is related to each part.

Your goal is to monitor these parameters at such a rate that you can be reasonably sure every part you are making and sending to your customers has received the ideal processing parameters.

In looking at the parameter level, the pyramid concept at the individual part level (see Chapter 4) works extremely well with some minor modifications, including some evaluation criteria that do not apply and have been removed. For the balance, the criteria are carried over without change and it's shown in Figure 6.2. The steps to rate the devices that monitor the parameters are just a smaller version of the steps we used to rate the devices for the part level (see Chapter 4). You start by looking at the foundation

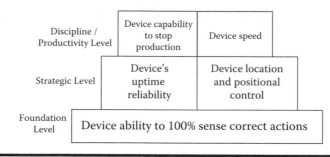

Figure 6.2   SET device rating pyramid for parameters.

level of the pyramid, determining how simple the device is and how good it is at detecting the correct actions. At the strategic level, determine whether the devices are reliable and placed in the correct spot. Last, at the discipline and productivity levels, is the device tied into production and can a bad part be prevented from escaping?

Monitoring Parameters

Figure 6.3 shows the rating scores for devices that are relevant to the parameter monitoring. By using the numbering system, the manufacturing engineers have a consistent means to assess the relative capability of each device and look for the ones that optimize the control of the elements that is critical to operational success. The method you will follow is as follows:

1. Rate every device used to monitor the process using the parameter rating matrix in Figure 6.2.
2. Do the best you can to maximize your score within your budget.
3. Define for each workstation the ideal value-added parameters needed for success.
4. Find devices that can constantly monitor those parameters.

Involving the Entire Facility in SET

SET will extend to many departments and staffs. Ideal methods or devices may be built into the equipment from the original manufacturers, which involves purchasing. Injection molding machines, for example, with built-in temperature and pressure controls are typically included in the purchase order. The placement of devices on equipment may need coordination with the safety or human relations

			Criteria	Score
Foundation Level			**1. Simplicity and Ability**	
		Robust	Simple — uses low-tech shelf items	2
		Capable	Complicated — Needs technical support	1
Strategic Level			**3. Devices Uptime & Reliability**	
		Robust	Downtime less than 10 minutes per quarter	2
		Capable	Downtime less than 10 minutes per month	1
			5. Positional	
		Robust	Confirms success in the station	2
		Capable	Confirmation is done in the subsequent station	1
		Max Risk	Last station (multiply total score by)	.66
		Risk	Two stations before last (multiply total by)	.85
Discipline/Speed Level			**6. Stop Production**	
		Robust	Operation stopped for correction or immediate marking of defect and immediate containmentinto a controlled condition	2
		Capable	Operation stopped for human Intervention	1
			10. Device Speed	
		Robust	Devices do not slow cycle time	2
		Capable	Devices slow cycle time less than 5%	1

Figure 6.3   Parameter rating matrix.

staff. And on and on. Involving your entire facility is critical if you want to succeed with SET.

The SET Summary Form

The information you accumulated in this chapter needs to be placed in the SET summary form. Look at Figure 6.4, where Columns 9, 10, and 11 are place holders for the information you just obtained. Column 9 is for the value-adding energy type and amount. Column 10 is the monitoring device you plan to use. Column 11 is the sum of the scores that the device possesses from the parameter rating matrix in Figure 6.3.

The last element on the form is simple math. You will calculate the Success Likelihood Number as the product of the part level score (Column 6), the set-up level score (Column 8), the parameter-level score (Column

Operation	Part Level					Set-up Level			Parameter Level				Success Likelihood Number
	Key Feature	Ideal Action	Target	Device	Part Level Score	Method	Set-up Level Score		Parameter Target Amount	Device	Part Level Score	P O S	
												1	
												1	
												1	
												1	
												1	
												1	
												1	
												1	
												1	
												1	
												.85	
												.85	
												.66	
						Column 6	Column 8		Column 9	Column 10	Column 11	Column 12	Column 13

Figure 6.4   The SET summary form.

11), and the positional control factor (Column 12). This number is placed in Column 13 as the Success Likelihood Number.

Note: Column 12 is the positional control column. Recall the discussion in Chapter 4 that the most risky operation to your customers is the last position on the line. A mistake at the end can only be found by your customer. To systematically drive stronger elements of control, the last three stations on any line have a built-in numbering handicap. Without these controls on all three of the last operations, the Success Likelihood Number has a reduction of 34%, while a lack of control on the two operations preceding the last operation diminishes the Success Likelihood Number by 15%. The reason you want to do this is to bring close attention to importance of the last three operations and the last operation in particular.

When the SET summary form is complete for an entire production line, with details at each individual operation, management can concentrate its energy on the jobs with the least support. The completed form will also stimulate engineers to balance their efforts in a strategic and cost-effective manner.

Key Points

- At the parameter level, you are monitoring the sources of energy that create your value-add.
- The addition of value is what your customers are truly buying from you—the action that you must do perfectly in order to satisfy your customers and maximize your profits.
- There are a relatively few different types of energy, and all are relatively easy to monitor.
- The best means of monitoring is to have the equipment makers of your value-adding energy provide built-in monitoring devices; include monitoring devices in your specifications.
- The culmination of the process is the creation of the SET summary form and the calculation of the Success Likelihood Number for each operation.
- Management can use the SET summary form to help drive resources to the workstations with the greatest amount of risk to customers.

PERFECTING AND MONITORING YOUR ERROR-PROOFING DEVICES

Chapter 7

Designing Parts That Are Device Compatible

Success Every Time (SET) involves focusing your efforts to help operators do the correct process every time. SET always involves a number of error-proofing devices that monitor the work, but the design of parts also plays a big role in helping operators succeed. Hundreds of time-saving features can be built into the design of the component parts at no cost, thus making the life of the production operators simpler. You just need to systematically think about the interface of parts and devices. This chapter tells you how.

Understanding Key Identifying Features

When selecting and positioning, operators need to be able to know which is the right part and which way that part should be oriented. These key identifying features (also called *special characteristics*) are extremely valuable for the entire processing at that workstation because the characteristics serve as reference points that your tooling operators can look for.

I believe there should be key error-proofing features on each and every part used at the workstation as well. Design engineers should identify a unique physical property on *each* part that can be mechanically identified and used as a reference point during production, to assist in the selection of the parts and their positioning and orientation as the parts pass through the workstation. There are a few exceptions where introducing a unique physical characteristic for each part is difficult, but for 99% of all parts, this is not only possible, but easy.

Keep in mind that unique identifying features should be called out on drawings and part specifications and treated as a critical characteristic. If any design change occurs that affects the key identifying feature, all the stakeholders need to agree to study the change and identify an alternative key error-proofing feature for use in processing.

Creating a key identifying feature is simple to do. You can place uniquely sized holes or tabs in parts, in out-of-the-way places that have no direct impact to the customer but provide a reference point for the production people.

With a key identifying feature for each part, the operator part selection and part orientation is made much easier. Some of the basic points to consider in defining these features are as follows. Effective key identifying features:

■ Make the part's unique feature extremely obvious to the operators.
■ Make physical detection easy.
■ Locate the feature to make it an advantage during the production processing and invisible during the customer use.
■ Allows operators to tell at a distance of ten feet the difference between two parts that have a similar appearance.

In product design, the entire effort is tremendously simplified when parts have features that are easily detectable. The shape of the part is the single most precious element to do this. Many parts have a unique shape and you can see the difference between one part and another, and you can easily tell whether a part is upside down or misoriented. For these parts, the features are already present: all we need to do is to use them. However, many parts are very similar in appearance and shape, and the unique features are either very discrete or (most often) just not designed in. On these similar looking or somewhat symmetrical parts, the design of each unique characteristic needs to use identifying holes with different sizes, shapes, and locations placed in a flat area of the part. Wherever possible, also use two holes of different sizes and place them in a nonsymmetric pattern. This chapter briefly touches on these and other ways to drive SET into your product design.

Method 1: Use Holes

Using holes as the primary method is based on the logic that:

1. Holes use less material and over time can save you money.
2. Holes eliminate mass and in most situations, lighter is better.
3. Holes can easily be confirmed by using fixed pins in parts and fixtures and are 100% reliable and implementable—the least expensive method.
4. Holes of different sizes can help people with the proper orientation of the part (also using pins of appropriate size).
5. Nonsymmetrical holes can help distinguish right side up from upside down.

Method 2: Use Notches on the Sides of Parts

While the primary method is to use holes, a close second is the use of notches on the sides of the parts. For notches, it is important to recognize that the notches need to be quite distinct as well. Ideally, there would be three notches, on different edges of the part, and all should be located in very odd locations on the edge following the idea of *10–45–75*.

The first notch should be located in the first 10% of the length of the part. The second notch would be near midpoint (45%), and the third notch located three-quarters of the way (75%) along the third edge. At the same time, the notches need to have different sizes and shapes. Having a rectangular notch on one side, a triangular notch on side two, and a circular notch on side three makes the placement and shape a strategic advantage in the SET process. Placing a notch on the sides in this manner:

1. Uses less material, which saves mass and cost.
2. The notches can easily be matched with tabs from mating parts for both proper positioning as well as correct selection of parts.
3. The notches can also be confirmed by using fixed tabs in the fixtures.
4. The different shapes and locations can assist in proper orientation.
5. The 10–45–75 approach makes the edges so uniquely obvious and different that the odds of the notches matching up are negligible.

Method 3: Use Tabs on Parts

The third most reliable method is to use tabs on the parts, again in a nonsymmetrical pattern and using different sizes and shapes. Tabs on parts are extremely easy to sense by interference-type devices like pins, switches, and bars. You may be thinking, "Why are tabs any different than holes and notches?" The difference is that tabs stick out and have a tendency to break off or can easily be cut off or trimmed. However, the tab approach is very smart in many applications and should be used if the holes or notch approaches don't seem appropriate.

While there are other features people can use as keys, like electrical resistance, material density, electromagnetic properties, and material density, physical features tend to be the best. Why? These are the most simple and can be matched up with the more simple and robust devices that you can place into the production stream.

Key Points

- Having a systematic process to consider time-saving and quality-improving features into parts is a no-cost strategic advantage.
- Design into the parts key identifying features that make each individual part obviously unique from all other parts in your plant:
  - Use uniquely placed holes
  - Use notches in the sides of the parts
  - Use tabs on the edge
- Think about feature placement using the 10–45–75 rule:
  - On three different edges, place one key identifying feature at the 10% point, one at the 45% point, and the last at the 75% point
  - Recognize that three points make a plane, which helps in proper positioning

Chapter 8

Investing in Your Devices

If a company goes through all the trouble of investing in error-proofing, you might think it'd be obvious that they would want to invest in their devices. Unfortunately, many don't. In order to have Success Every Time (SET), your error-proofing devices need a support system that delivers long term results. Your investment must include a set of support mechanisms that ensure your error-proofing devices are working the way they should.

Your investment in devices must include four essential elements that will cause the error-proofing devices to live and provide the type of excellent performance that everyone seeks. They need to be looked at as interconnected building blocks.

- Device robustness.
- Ongoing device verification.
- Device disengagement control.
- Consequence to defective parts.

In this chapter, I look at each element, help you understand the significance of each, and know why they are important. These support mechanisms are illustrated in Figure 8.1.

Robustness of the Device

SET devices need to be capable of helping people see the difference between doing a job right versus wrong. A robust device works 100% of the

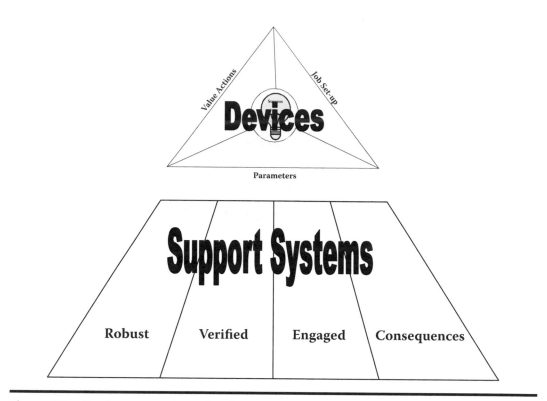

Figure 8.1 Device support mechanisms.

time, helps people do what is right and is capable of distinguishing the ideal proper actions from anything else. Through this capability you can control the quality level of your production and sort out parts that are on the borderline between good and bad. They can help people make the decision to proceed with production or to stop.

This is a tall order. Know what is right, be able to see it every time, and never miss.

How do you evaluate a device against this need for infallibility? What is a good device versus one that is marginal? How do you know that it works, especially for the marginal parts that are produced due to normal variation?

Most people look at an error-proofing device and assume it works. The unfortunate fact is that very few people apply any scientific method to evaluate the devices against solid criteria. In reality, they assume the device works but never really test it to find out.

Error-proofing devices are the most economical tool you can find that can prevent you from making waste (scrap) and provide your customers with 100% defect-free parts. They are the best filter you have to both save money and improve quality. Although most people overlook this aspect, error-proofing devices are literally gauges. Their job is to differentiate between good and not good, and do so 100% of the time. If that is the challenge, what is the test?

We find there are four key aspects to the robustness of the device.

Does the Device Work?

The first aspect is, does it work for all conditions and can it detect whether the process is being performed properly? The device must be capable to determine 100% of the time that the individual components are in the exact correct location and that the value-add functions are done exactly right. Remember that you are looking for a cost-effective means of picking needles out of haystacks. You are seeking to identify the 2 out of 10,000 parts that are not perfect and help your operators identify those parts before any more value is added to them. This aspect is the heart of SET. You are looking at the point where the true risk is. Anything that is missed generally ends up in the hands of the customer and if the product is not right, they are the ones who get hurt first. It always reflects your bottom line in either less revenue (because you lose repeat customers) or higher warranty costs.

Can a Step be Skipped?

The second aspect is whether the process is adequately planned such that you cannot complete the process if a step is skipped. This isn't so much about operators intentionally skipping a step as it is that people just plain forget. When you are in a routine process and get interrupted, it is easy to forget where you were. Have you ever been doing a daily task like ironing clothes or cleaning the dishes, and then the phone rings and you go off to answer it? On coming back to the original task, you may forget where you were, forget to unplug the iron, or whatever. In a routine production environment, this same situation happens every day. The good thing is that a well-designed device can spot where people left off and make sure they do the right things or see the oversight in a simple and effective manner.

Do Operators Like the Device?

Evaluating the devices up front on this aspect is a minimal requirement to make. The key is to test the devices and make sure they do what you want and that the people like them and see them as a positive. The influence of the operator cannot be overemphasized. Think about operators' typical work life. They usually perform a repetitive task and do it correctly 98 to 99% of the time. In pursuing SET, you are going after that final 1 or 2%. If the device can keep pace with the operator and does not add work, the operator will want to keep the device around. On the other hand, if the device slows the operator down or adds work, the operator will be disadvantaged for the 98 or 99% of his day when he or she was doing great without the device. If the device gets in the way, many operators will figure out a means to get rid of the obstacle the device imposes. This is the worst of all worlds: not only have you wasted the money invested in the device, you also are running with a known vulnerability. All of this is the result of incomplete upfront planning that did not fully or properly evaluate the operator's preferences.

Operator friendliness is a common term in the auto industry that describes how production operators perceive the tools they are given. If there is a tool that operators like, the tool is described as operator friendly. We all know of tools or tasks that the operators dislike or are operator unfriendly, and you can understand that the operators are motivated to find ways around these uncomfortable elements.

The most frequent failure of an error-proofing device does not come from the device or its reliability, but from the operators who use them. It does not matter how clever the engineer or how sophisticated the overall controls and technology, every device can be disengaged or bypassed by operators, if they want to. It may take some time, it may take some effort, but if they want to find a way around the device, they will.

The engineers who design error-proofing devices do the best they can to create devices that perform a task. The devices are then installed and turned over to the production operators. These operators then work with these devices every day. They learn the tasks of their jobs and run their cycles in the same manner almost every time. If something unusual happens, management wants the devices to perform a reminder function and help operators follow the sequences that creates perfect parts every time. This is the goal. Error-proofing devices are an assist to the operators to perform the job successfully every time.

In situations where devices are seen as a hindrance of some type, operators become motivated to overcome the hindrance. The degree of their actions to do something about it is in direct correlation to how well they like the error-proofing devices. If they like the devices and see them

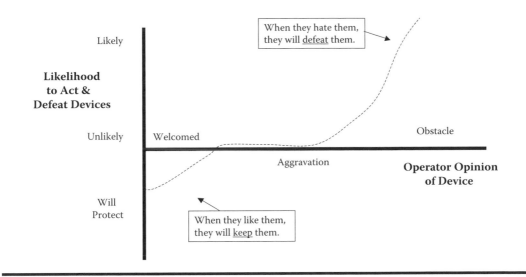

Figure 8.2   Operator motivation to defeat devices.

as an asset, they will make sure the devices work. By the same token, if they see the devices as obstacles, they will work to find a way around it. This concept is illustrated in Figure 8.2. Not all operators will do this, but when you have a device that isn't accepted by an operator, you always run this risk.

The secret to winning in this situation is asking, "How can you address the motivation?" The operator friendliness evaluation is a method to review the devices from an operator's perspective in order to understand and see the issues. It essentially comes down to reviewing the devices from the perspective of the normal distribution of your workforce, and having regular operators evaluate each device against typical operator concerns. Look at Figure 8.3, which is a simple method to secure input from the most common cross section of operators.

To properly conduct the evaluation, a little upfront planning is useful to make sure the needs of all types of operators are evaluated. Your workforce is probably comprised of a set of men and women of various ages and skills, some left handed, some shorter, and so on. It is a typical mix of people, all coming to work to earn a living for their families. So, first off, you need to make sure devices are usable by people of all sizes and characteristics, and then you need to deploy a process to have the devices tested by the various groups. Establish a set of operators of all sizes and characteristics, in order to give yourself a chance to see the issues and concerns under a controlled setting. Some example characteristics are:

	Safety		Effort		Speed		Comments
	OK	Concern	OK	Concern	OK	Concern	
Male							
Female							
Right Handed							
Left Handed							
Short							
Tall							

Figure 8.3   Operator friendliness evaluation form.

Male	*Female*
Right handed	*Left handed*
New operator (less than 90 days)	*Experienced (more than 10 years)*
Tall (over 6′2″)	*Short (under 5′2″)*

Before starting, it is best to give the people a quick training session because they need to understand that their role as evaluators is to give you insights on how well the device will be perceived and used by operators just like them. You are asking them to let you know what and where the issues are. They also need to know that if they have ideas, you want to hear them because the devices are being installed to help them—and the company—win.

The operator friendliness evaluation process involves each selected person evaluating each device, which may take a few weeks. Each operator usually needs a few hours to get used to doing the jobs before they get a chance to actually do the error-proofing evaluation. The best approach is to select your evaluation pool of people, and then place each operator on each job for two days, and record their comments at the end.

In all evaluations, you'll want to include the operators who will perform the job most of the time, but you want these operators to run a range of size, shape, and characteristics.

The rest is relatively simple. Find out what operators don't like, and act accordingly by redesigning the device.

Do All Value-Added Steps Have Devices?

The fourth element of robustness is that the SET device must impose consequences to the parts at key points related to the value-added steps. Let's face it; some operations add small increments of value, while other steps add significant value. Consider the simple example of baking cookies. The first few steps are combining the sugar, eggs, and flour, which are all relatively inexpensive. If you make a small mistake here, you can correct it rather inexpensively. Once the baking step happens, however, the cookies are converted from a state of batter into the final cookie state, and there is no turning back. The baking step, then, is the high value-add. Once you take that step, no corrections are economically feasible. If you make a mistake, you're better off throwing out the batch and starting over. But if the mixing was done properly and the baking settings and time are correct, you succeed. In a nutshell, then, the simple and inexpensive steps must be done correctly before you take the high value-add step.

Ongoing Verification of the Device

Most companies understand the relevance of checking to make sure the devices are working and they conduct tests on a regular basis to confirm this. What is surprising, though, is how often management doesn't think about this step hard enough. Checking to make sure the devices are working is smart business. Doing the verification quickly and effectively is even smarter.

To do it right, a time efficient test needs to be in place for the operators to quickly confirm the device is working. But quick is a relative term. Five minutes could be quick to some companies and extremely long for others. In the auto industry, we generally produce one car every minute in every assembly plant. Verifying the error-proofing devices and consuming five minutes is very expensive. Five minutes per shift means fifteen cars per day at 220 production days per year amounts to over 3,000 units per year selling at $15,000, which rolls up into a revenue loss of $4.5 million. This cost could be too much to absorb, so getting the verification done quicker than five minutes is smart business. A general rule of thumb is that a verification activity should take less than two normal production cycles, especially in a mass production setting. And this is just a quick test to confirm the devices are working as they should.

In addition to the speed element, the tests need to check for proper identification of the good as well as proper determination of the bad. This seems so logical but people perform only one check or the other. Let me provide an example. Imagine you have a bracket that has a critical hole in it and you provide a pin (the device) that looks for adequate clearance for the hole. In this case you are checking for a minimum size hole and your test matrix would include looking for parts with the hole missing. This test would be correct if the only abnormal condition was a missing hole or a hole that is too small.

On the other end of the spectrum, you may have a hole that is completely too large and can cause your product to be unacceptable. If you do not have a test that looks for oversized holes, your test matrix would accept a part that is not good. So the trick is to look at your testing plan and provide means to test more than one dimension if necessary, as shown in Figure 8.4.

Most companies check error-proofing devices by passing a part across the fixture to see whether it works. If they are testing for a specific feature, the company will get a part with that characteristic, pass that part across the fixture, and see if the device catches that it works.

What is important to note is that these bad parts (called golden samples, red rabbits, and error-proofing confirmation parts) are extremely critical to the success of the company. They need to be treated like gauges and have a regular replacement program. Passing a part over a fixture causes contact with the physical parts, which causes friction and wear and tear. The bad parts, therefore, wear out and need to be checked and replaced periodically, just like the brakes or windshield wipers on your car.

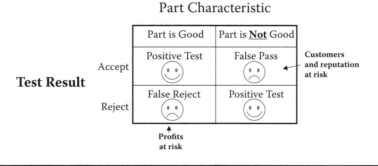

Figure 8.4   Test integrity matrix.

Device Disengagement Control

Device disengagement control is interesting because it involves planning for the times when you are the most vulnerable. When the devices are properly up and running, you are in a state of minimal risk. If a mistake happens or a deviation is present, devices will do their thing and make the situation obvious. You will find the substandard part and have the chance to respond.

Unfortunately, the world throws unexpected situations at you and from time to time devices become disengaged and get turned off. The situations happen in two typical categories:

- **Controlled disengagement:** The devices are turned off with a simultaneous installation of a backup system.
- **Uncontrolled disengagement:** Devices are turned off without backup.

Let's look at these two situations in a little more detail.

Controlled Disengagement

With *controlled disengagement,* the organization is experiencing a situation where they must temporarily turn off the device in order to continue production. For example, imagine you need to make an engineering change to the design of the part and you add a feature that interferes with one of your existing SET devices. If you don't have enough time to modify your error-proofing devices, you may need to temporarily pull the devices out of the production process until you can re-establish total control at a later time. As an example, if a key feature is a tab on the outside edge of a part, and a new mating component is designed and now is touching the tab and causing a rattle or squeak, you may need to remove the original tab in order to protect the quality of the overall product.

Companies employing SET find a different identification feature and create a different tab in a different area, so that the error-proofing situation is restored with a different device in place. Although the ideal state is all these things come together all at the same time, in reality, they don't. Sometimes, the timing prioritizes the new design change in the product but the related error-proofing devices for the production process are implemented later on. The net result is that you end up running without the devices operating as planned.

Additionally, there are times when the devices are not working correctly. You may have wear and tear on the devices, and they may start to generate false signals. You know the parts are right and the operators are processing them correctly, but the error-proofing device is kicking a good part out as a bad part. The best case is to stop everything, fix the device, and go on. Yet there are times when taking the time to fix the device is in direct conflict with customer demands, so management is faced with running production with a higher level of quality risk.

These scenarios are very common events and need to be planned for because they do occur. Whenever you have risk, the smart thing to do is to provide a reasonable countermeasure for the risk and to do it in a disciplined and methodical manner. This method typically involves the following steps:

1. **Structure the decision to disengage.** In this step, the management group (usually production, maintenance, and the quality staff) discusses the trade-offs, determines the expected duration of the exposure, and creates action plans to reinstate proper control.

2. **Make a provision for backup.** During the exposed period, another confirmation must take place. Have operators take a special action, such as marking the part as a physical confirmation that they looked at the specific area of risk.

3. **Make the disengagement visible to management.** This is simple charting and management. Posting a list on the wall with the temporary conditions allows management to conduct backup checks as well as expedite the proper final solution.

4. **Begin a controlled return to normal.** Once the remedy is in place, management needs to provide reasonable confirmation steps that the new (or repaired) device is working. In most cases, the backup checks need to stay in place for at least one day while the new device is present and active. Here's why: in normal production, a ramp-up period occurs during which any new tools, devices, and people have the opportunity to employ normal learning curves; that is, they have the time to notice things. When a device is disengaged and then reintroduced, there is no learning curve available. The device is required to immediately produce at the normal production speed, in essence going from zero to full speed immediately. Placing a redundant check during this period is just plain smart. It gives you the chance to confirm the device's capability in a controlled manner.

Uncontrolled Disengagement

Uncontrolled disengagement involves situations where the SET device becomes nonfunctional and no backup support mechanism is put into place. There are situations in which uncontrolled disengagement has occurred and in those cases, a strategic set of actions is necessary.

Uncontrolled disengagement can happen during the unnoticed and unexpected failure of an error-proofing device. For example, if a pin is used to check the presence of a hole and the pin breaks off, there is no feature to check for the hole. Perhaps in the next hour or next shift, somebody notices the situation and action is taken to reestablish proper control.

There is another category of uncontrolled disengagement and that is of operators turning the devices off because they are getting in the way. This situation happens all too often. If you are an operator and the device is slowing you down or causing you grief, you are motivated to find a way to get around it, especially when the problem situation happens rarely and the operator believes he or she will notice a problem if it does occur. So the operator shuts off the device (and believe me, an operator can always find a way to override or disengage a device).

For uncontrolled disengagements, the method to counter the situation is similar to the controlled approach, with a few added steps.

1. **Understand the driving forces.** Why did the device become inactive? If it broke, find a means for preventive maintenance and get the countermeasure in place. If the operator turned it off, find out why and address the design of the device to remove the disengagement motivation.
2. **Contain the suspect production.** If the batch of parts produced with the controls removed is still in the plant, it makes sense to perform a redundant inspection. Find the parts that were produced between the last known time the device was properly functioning and the time the disengagement was discovered, and reinspect them. This is normally a way to protect your reputation with your customers.
3. **Enhance the verification.** When such a situation is discovered, you are given an opportunity to strengthen your system. Because the deployment of devices is usually standardized, your plant may have the same device in multiple locations. Set up a means to check that all the devices of similar features remain up and running properly. If it happened once, it probably will happen again.

Bad Part Control (Consequences to Defective Parts)

After you put all the work into setting up the error-proofing devices and making sure they work right, when the system works and kicks out a bad part, you have to retain control of that bad part and see that it doesn't end up in the hands of a customer.

This element of investing in your devices may be the most important of them all. When you have identified a defective part, how can you make the system work in such a way that you either correct the part and make it right or control the part and dispose of it so it cannot escape your plant. It's like a hospital handling people with contagious diseases. You want to heal the person and get him or her back to total health, but you also want a total quarantine of the diseased cells so that they can never escape into the world. This is just the way is has to be. When a problem is found, it must be totally resolved, every time, with no release of any bad parts into the market.

Here are some simple steps to take to ensure that bad parts are controlled. Each is discussed in detail in the following sections.

1. Immediate identification and immediate confirmed remedy wherever possible.
2. Immediate identification with appropriate marking when immediate remedy is not possible.
3. Immediate quarantine and removal from the work area of the properly marked components.
4. Controlled handling of the parts to a tear down and data collection area.
5. Complete disposition (confirmed repair, proper salvage, or total scrapping).

Let's look at these elements in a little more detail.

Immediate Identification and Confirmed Remedy

When a mistake occurs, the system immediately notifies the operator, who makes the appropriate correction, allowing the person to complete the task and go about their day. Think of it in everyday terms: When you go to the automatic teller machine, the machine gets your account number from the computer files and asks you for your personal identification number. If you type in the wrong number, the machine gives you an error message and gives you a chance to retype the code. You made the mistake, you were notified immediately, and you can correct the error immediately so you can complete your transaction. It is immediate, it is correctible, and it fits your need of protection from theft, and the recognition that you may make a mistake now and then.

In producing parts, if you didn't load a part correctly (let's say you put it in upside down), the system would, ideally, notify you. You would then make the correction and put the part in right, and you would be making great parts and go about your day thinking little about the device. This is by far the best scenario you can establish. The system can only make correct parts, and if human error occurs that error is immediately corrected, allowing only perfect parts to pass.

Immediate Identification with Immediate Marking

Whenever an immediate correction is not possible, you want to mark the part as being defective and note what is wrong! You can't just find a defective part and throw it into a box or lay it aside. You must take the time to describe what is wrong.

The problem with not marking a bad part is twofold. First, there are times that the bad part looks very similar to the perfect ones, so someone might overlook the defect, put it back in the system, and send it to a customer, thus opening another opportunity for ruining the company's reputation in the eyes of the customer. It is one thing to let a bad part out that you could not see; it is a totally different and embarrassing situation when you let out a part you knew was bad.

Second, you may identify a bad part but you don't seize the opportunity to immediately identify what is wrong, leaving the detective work to other operators later on in the process. When operators start the process to address the bad part, the first step is to find out what is wrong. Most of the time, the operator does it with some type of inspection, but it makes so much more sense for the operator who first found the defect to make an appropriate mark and note what is wrong (right there on the part) giving an adequate description of the malady. Many production workers, as well as management, think this step takes too much time and reduces overall output. In reality, I've found that taking this step actually reduces time spent on the problem by 75% and leads to better repairs and analysis. Good part marking lowers cost and risk tremendously.

Come up with codes for common defects and have operators mark the part with the code (typically five to ten seconds per piece). If you need to, attach a wire tag and write some message that may take ten to fifteen more seconds for each part. This is a tiny amount of time when you consider the possible consequences if you don't do this immediate marking. On the other hand, if the repair person gets a box of defective unmarked parts, he or she has to spend time discovering what was wrong with them. Not only does this take a great deal of time, but he or she may not find the defect at all—or find only one when there were two or three defects in the part.

Use a tagging or marking system that:

1. Is easy and quick for your operators.
2. Is hard for your downstream production operators to remove and prevents them from adding value until remedied.
3. Provides quick and direct information to the repair people.
4. Is relatively easy for the repair people to remove following proper handling of the part.

One additional note: instead of using wire twist tags, use plastic zip strips that the repair person can cut off or recycle after removing with a simple tool. You don't want to use anything that is very expensive, but recyclable tags are a great marker because they're easy to get on and hard to remove without a simple tool. Then, you just give the tool to the qualified repair person, and you have a total system. It's simple, inexpensive, and comprehensive. The key is to do the marking immediately and thoroughly and set your associates up to maximize quality and minimize cost.

Immediate Quarantine and Removal from the Work Area of the Properly Marked Components

When a part is found that cannot be immediately repaired, it needs to go somewhere—and fast. When a bad parts comes along, it needs to be marked and "BAM" (like Emeril Lagasse says), it needs to get out of the production area. Provide boxes in a strategic location to store these parts, and put the container near enough to the operator to get to it quickly, yet far enough away to get the questionable part totally out of the "known good part" production flow. This is known as a quarantine of the part.

The worst thing would be to allow the re-introduction of a known bad part to get out of a box and to a customer. After spending all the time and effort to find a bad part, you let it out anyway. Logic would tell you, if you let a known bad part escape, you would have been better off not having the error-proofing in the first place. You have wasted your money.

Many companies use red boxes that get placed under the table, giving the operators a place to store the defective parts. Some companies like to make the waste more visible than that. Instead of placing the bad part under the table, they create some type of hook device that hangs the part up above the station so everyone can see it. If you have a choice, placing the defects into highly visible racks or hooks is the best method. When people see the defects they start the problem-solving and corrective action process and begin to understand the cause, accelerating the time to get a more robust method into place.

One of the best solutions was described to me by Jeff Bobcean, an automotive industry quality change agent working on a project with an electronics company. The activity at the plant included a place to stack the defective parts on a carousel, with a designated place for the most common defects. When the operator found a problem part, he or she spun the carousel to find the matching defect and placed the part in the designated space. It made the defect instantly obvious to everyone, and it simultaneously provided an instant Pareto chart of the defects, an instant count, and a signal to people where vulnerability was present.

When you quarantine the defective parts, it does not mean you hide them. In fact, hiding defects is really the last thing you want to do. You really want to get the defective parts out of the way of the production people and make the defect visible so that the support system can come and provide help, if required. By quarantine, I just mean getting the parts totally out of the stream of good production and into a state of control for proper disposition.

After quarantine, the defective part must be removed in a timely way. Here's an analogy: in my lifetime, I've never been subjected to a garbage strike. I have heard about them in major cities like New York and Chicago, but where I have lived, I have never experienced one. Instead, the garbage collector comes once a week and provides an awesome service to take our waste to the dump. The value to us is better health, a more pleasant neighborhood, and so on. The process we rely on is the regularly scheduled pickup by a service with the proper equipment to move it away.

During the big city garbage strikes, I cannot imagine the mess and the chaos. The first thing has to be the overflowing volume of the trash. At first, it starts piling up alongside the regular trash cans. Next, the items start to decompose and the people start moving the trash away from their house and start moving it into the street. As time goes on, trash continues to pile up and the attitude of the community and the health of everybody goes into a regular state of decline and you are into a bona fide state of pandemonium. Everything gets out of control, and the entire community health is at stake. Even when the strike is resolved, cleaning up the matter is even worse. The normal system is able to handle a certain volume per week, but this temporary overload has to be dealt with while the normal production of waste continues. It must be a disaster.

This is similar to handling defects created in production. The disposal must have a regular cycle (I highly recommend collecting the defective parts twice per shift) and be performed by a team that is dedicated to the effort with enough equipment and capacity to get the job done. These people need to know that removing these defective parts is like handling the health of the company. They must secure the parts on a scheduled basis (work overtime, if necessary, so a build up does not occur) and properly remove them from the production area. This is needed for the health of the plant to remain strong. Perhaps you have been in plants where the scrap is not handled in this type of manner. The defective parts build up, they start exceeding the space dedicated to hold them, the pile of parts starts to become a magnet for other trash, and suddenly a huge problem develops due to neglect.

For a company to be healthy, regular removal of the quarantined bad parts is needed. To do that properly, you need a person or team assigned to follow a mandatory schedule and get the defective parts away from the good ones in a timely and effective manner.

Controlled Handling of the Parts to a Tear Down and Data Collection Area

After defective parts are removed, you need to do something with them. To my knowledge, there are only two scenarios: nonrisk components (scrap the parts) and components with some risk (rework, salvage, or repair the parts). From a quality point of view, scrapping the parts is the best. Parts that are made during the production process the first time are always better than any part that has to be double handled or re-processed. So if a part is not perfect the first time through the production line or area, scrap the part.

Unfortunately, the world is not that simple. As people work on products, they invest time and materials to convert parts from raw materials into products that delight customers. The more work that is needed, the greater the value invested; until you reach a point where scrapping the part becomes an illogical option. Consider a television set that costs $500. People make printed circuit boards that get attached to picture tubes, wires, and speakers and are placed in a plastic case, ready for purchase. If the last step is to place the TV into the case and a $5 speaker gets damaged in the process, it is hard for the company to justify throwing out a $500 TV when the $5 speaker can be reliably repaired. The repair decision boils down to economic risk and reward.

For this TV set, the decision to repair the speaker would be appropriate, especially if you have a qualified repair process and a solid method to test the repair. Unfortunately, in the production world, there are too many situations where the decision to repair or scrap is not supported by a well-considered analysis of risk and return. It is left in the hands of the repair people to decide, and most conscientious repair people will decide to repair more than management really wants them to—that is, more than the risk and reward can justify.

To properly perform a repair, consider a few items:

1. **Is the risk worth the benefit?** Repaired parts are never as good as new parts. What is the economic point at which scrapping is a better option than repairing it? Most companies do not define this point.
2. **Is the repair person and repair process capable of making a great part from the defective one?** Most of the time this is an "assumed" item, so ask yourself the question, "What data do I have to know that the repair process is capable?"
3. **Is there an adequately robust test of the repair process to help you isolate the customer from the defect?** This is what your long term success hinges on. Do people like what you make or will they have a bad experience?

Management needs to make a scrap-versus-repair policy instead of making it a decision of the repair person.

So what is the rule of thumb or formula for the economic risk versus reward decision? I don't have one. The decision will stem from the confidence you have in the repair process versus the potential risk of harm in the use by the customer. Replacing a two-cent spring in a ballpoint pen is something I would do, because the risk to the customer is low and my confidence in the repair is very high. If the exact same two-cent spring was inside a seatbelt buckle and secured a human being in a car crash, I would throw the entire seat belt buckle away and avoid the risk of failure. It still is the same two-cent spring, but the relative risk is tremendously different.

In either scenario, the data from the scrap or repair activity is a goldmine of information that most people disregard. Knowledge of any part that is not right the first time through can enrich your long term profitability. In fact, tracking this data is the heart of Toyota's success. During my time at NUMMI I learned Toyota's basic cornerstone for success is "continuous improvement and the elimination of waste." In Toyota's system, having people see and understand the waste, and then turning people loose to eliminate the waste, is a perpetual economic engine for success. The parts that are kicked out as scrap hold the secrets to future success because you can find out what did not go right and which machines or operations yielded these defective parts. Whenever parts are kicked out for scrap or repair of any kind, the data must be tracked and resources applied to fix the problem. During the scheduled part removal and disposition, the data tracking cannot be ignored, as it is a key to greater profits. Either the defect collection person or the repair people need to track and report the data (daily) to help operators make the necessary adjustments and set them up to win.

Once you track the data, you can set up methods that eliminate this defect in the future. Fixing the production system in this way increases first-time yield (parts that come down the production line one time with perfect quality), increases profits due to less rework and scrap, and increases productivity. It is a win in all arenas.

Complete Disposition

The actions to repair, salvage, or scrap the defective part needs to be complete and fast. Quality engineers need to view the repair areas as complete factories, with controls that are more rigorous than the regular production areas.

In the production areas, the work is highly repeatable and predictable. In repair, there is a very high degree of craftsmanship, complexity, and variability. Most repair processes are a huge source of both cost savings (and thereby profits) but also potential customer risk. You want to place sophisticated and rigorous testing devices in the repair area, as well as redundantly that requires the repaired part to go through the repair tester as well as back through the production tester.

Whatever the means, the repair operation needs to be managed daily. Ideally, at the start of a shift, there are zero items in the repair queue, and

100% of the defective parts made during the shift are handled within the shift. They are either totally repaired or scrapped within the shift (with associated data collection). This may mean the repair person starts a little later than the balance of the team and stays over longer to clear out the parts made at the end of the shift. Some companies tolerate a small inventory of defective parts to go across shifts (for example, a maximum of three parts, properly marked) so that the repair person's hours match that of the regular shift. In any event, the purging of the defective parts must be done daily, just like removing the waste from a city. It has to be constant and must be considered a flow item; otherwise the health of the entire community starts to suffer. Complete disposition is crucial to successful error-proofing, but it is frequently seen as an afterthought and eventually causes a company to head toward significant financial losses.

Key Points

- Investing in devices maximizes the return on the investment in the devices.
- The basic elements of device investment are as follows:
  - Device robustness: How reliable are they to work 100% of the time?
  - Ongoing verification: Do people make sure the devices are working?
  - Disengagement control: If the device is turned off are backup checks provided?
  - Consequences to defective parts: When a part is "kicked out"—is the correction complete?
- A key focus is the perspective of the production operators: the best devices are the ones that operators welcome.
- Special attention needs to be placed on controlling any part the devices detect as improper:
  - The devices are designed to control the nonperfect situations
  - The system is telling people something is wrong
  - The worst situation you can have is letting a part flow to your customers when you knew something was wrong
- There is huge risk in incomplete repair or rework. Be very careful to have extremely solid control of all rework.

Chapter 9

Creating Great Devices, Placing Them, and Verifying Their Success

Working on achieving Success Every Time (SET) can be both immensely rewarding and mildly frustrating. There will be times that you just cannot come up with a device that can do what you want, within the budget that you have allocated. And even after you have devices in place, you have to make sure they work properly for a long time. This chapter shares a few tips and tricks that can help. The first section helps you define great devices and gives you a device rating matrix to ensure that your devices fall into this "great" category. The second, the stairway matrix, is a simple and effective way to identify the best places to position the devices. It is a means to help you place them in the production stream for maximum benefit.

The third, the device evaluation matrix, is an easy way to visually see how well protected your line is from potential errors as well as a way for plant managers to help his or her team enjoy the benefits the devices can deliver.

Designing Great Devices—and Rating Their Effectiveness

One of the toughest questions to answer about error-proofing devices was asked by Ping Zhang, a 20-year veteran manufacturing engineer who has also taught university-level courses: "How can you tell a good one from a great one? What are the criteria to determine good, better, and best?"

Great error-proofing devices do the following:

1. Great devices truly help operators do their job exactly right, each and very time.
2. Great devices earn a high rating based on the factors illustrated in Figure 9.1.

When you consider these factors, you are seeking devices that deliver the strongest combination of:

- **Simplicity:** The best devices are simple, inexpensive, and use the forces of nature.
- **Strategic elements:** The devices are welcomed by operators and work constantly.
- **Discipline:** They help people follow the correct and best standard work.
- **Productivity:** The devices maximize your company output.

The device rating matrix in Figure 9.1 is a method to rate each device based on these multiple factors. To use this rating matrix, each device receives points for each dimension listed with the goal of maximizing the score. This

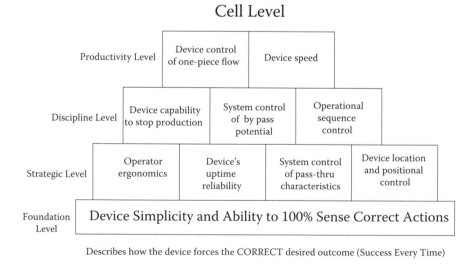

Figure 9.1   Device rating matrix.

method of rating the devices will drive your device selection to maximize the overall capability of the devices that you select. Keep in mind that error-proofing devices must satisfy multiple criteria. A great error-proofing device also needs to:

■ Be welcomed by the operators that use them.
■ Be fast and not slow down the cycle time.
■ Have outstanding uptime—ideally 100%.
■ Be 100% effective to sense the prescribed success feature.
■ Be as simple and inexpensive as possible.

When error-proofing devices meeting all of these criteria are in place, operators will recognize that the devices are an asset. To be totally effective, the set of devices needs to integrate with the flow of production; specifically, error-proofing devices need to influence the value-add step so that only success can occur. Error-proofing devices need to check the work of the operator and if everything is right, the value-add step needs to be allowed. But if something is not right, the device needs to affect the value-add step and stop it as soon as possible, ideally before the value gets added. The concept is illustrated as a flow diagram in Figure 9.2.

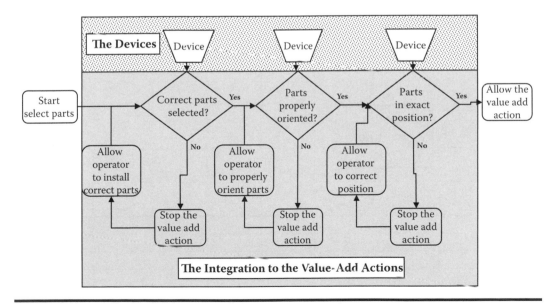

Figure 9.2   Device integration to value-add flow diagram.

The Stairway Matrix

The stairway matrix finds the most effective places to place your error-proofing devices in a visual manner. This is especially powerful in the planning stages of a new process because you can see where the devices are and you can intelligently and easily know where to concentrate your efforts.

The person who really got into the stairway matrix idea was Jeff Bobcean, a 30-year quality veteran with a gift of making theories practical, and a lot of the enrichment of the basic matrix goes to Jeff. The stairway matrix is a simple two-dimensional matrix in which operation stations are listed from start to finish on the top row of the matrix, and the same set of operations is listed from start to finish in the first column. The bottom of the matrix contains other reference information based on cost and risk. See Figure 9.3 for an example.

The cost information is shown in two levels: the cumulative value added to the product as it moves through production (level one), and the rough estimate of the error-proofing investment (level two). Because you

				Device Location					
Operation	10	20	30	40	50	60	70		Notes
10	IDEAL	STRONG	GOOD						
20		IDEAL	STRONG	GOOD		Ineffective Zone			
30			IDEAL	STRONG	GOOD				
40				IDEAL	STRONG	GOOD			
50		Precedes Opportunity Zone			IDEAL	STRONG	GOOD		
					Risk				
60						IDEAL	STRONG		
						High risk			
70							IDEAL		
							Maximum risk		
Cum value									
EP invest									
RPN									
Occurrence									
S.L.N.									

Figure 9.3   The stairway matrix.

are installing a number of devices at each station, the stairway matrix also shows the investment in error-proofing at each station, making it easy to see where you are spending your money.

In regard to the level of prevention, a place is set aside on the stairway matrix to record the Success Likelihood Number from the SET analysis. You are looking at typical problems that occur in production, and the SET method is aimed at creating more success. The most vulnerable stations, then, are the ones with the lowest success likelihood (lowest Success Likelihood Number), so that operation is the one we want to address the most.

As you look at the stairway matrix in Figure 9.3, notice how the stations are highlighted, with the greatest highlight on the station itself and the next two subsequent stations. For effective error-proofing, you want to find any mistake early. The ideal point is in the station of value-add, where the operator is required to make any necessary corrections to the production parts before the value-added energy is deployed. You either make the part right or not at all. If you can't provide means to detect the defective products in-station, the next best is the immediately successive operation. (In the SET approach, the last resort to find a mistake is two stations away from the point of value-add. If you wait too long and continue to add value to a defective product you are missing the real benefits.) Again, the products must be right or they don't get out. The last critical element in the stairway matrix is the highlighting of the last few stations. The only person who can find a mistake made by your last operator is the customer, which gives the last station by default the highest risk. (In fact, the last three stations as a group are higher risk than the others, with the last one representing the greatest risk.)

Take a look at Figure 9.3 again, noting the last three stations (Stations 50, 60, and 70). The most noteworthy station is the last one, Station 70. Mistakes made in this station that are allowed to pass through can be discovered only by the customer. Your last operator is the most critical. If this operator makes a mistake and a defective part is allowed to pass, you have no chance of finding the mistake and protecting your customer and your reputation. With this in mind, the strategic move is to increase your focus on every last operation in your facility.

While not quite as vulnerable, the two stations preceding the last one (in Figure 9.3, they are Stations 50 and 60) have limited chances to identify defects. For this reason, the SET method highlights the last three stations of any production process as the most risky. The stairway matrix highlights this risk and places it in front of you for an intelligent decision.

Device Confirmation Matrix

In my experience, error-proofing devices tend to work pretty well. The biggest problem is when you don't have a proactive method to drive device implementation or when you give only superficial nurturing to make sure they are healthy and continue to work.

Here's a nonmanufacturing example: my wife and I enjoy wine. We have gone to many wine regions and we have had the great fortune to talk to wine makers. Our favorite is the team of Squire and Suzy Fridell of Glen Lyon Vineyards in the Sonoma Valley. Just for fun, Cindy and I spent a vacation day working at the vineyard during the crush, which is the day they pick the grapes and start crushing them to start the winemaking process. We were astonished at the absolute quality of the grapes we were processing—each one seemed to be perfect. Being in the vineyard, we could see that the winemaking process actually started during the planting of the vines and continued during the meticulous care and nurturing during the growing season and harvest. In Squire Fridell's words, "Making wine is easy. Making great wine involves hard work." Until that visit, we could not appreciate the constant attention to detail that is needed in order to produce a truly great product.

The same thing goes with error-proofing. The devices are the vines in a winery. If you leave them on their own, they will do the best they can. But if you care for and nurture them, and give them what they need, they will return the favor to you with a harvest of great parts.

In the world of error-proofing, you need people to go out among the devices, regularly monitor them, and tend to their good health. As discussed in Chapter 7, error-proofing devices need the following points of care:

- Device reliability.
- Ongoing device verification.
- Device disengagement control.
- Consequence to the parts.

These elements need to be viewed as the water, soil, sunshine, and fertilizer to keep the devices healthy. Just like the vineyard master has pruning shears, irrigation equipment, and tools to loosen the soil and pull out the weeds, it is useful for the quality staff to have tools to make sure the error-proofing devices are working.

Operation & Device	Reliability	Verify	Disengage	Consequence	Comments
	O△X	O△X	O△X	O△X	
	O△X	O△X	O△X	O△X	
	O△X	O△X	O△X	O△X	
	O△X	O△X	O△X	O△X	
	O△X	O△X	O△X	O△X	
	O△X	O△X	O△X	O△X	
	O△X	O△X	O△X	O△X	
	O△X	O△X	O△X	O△X	

Rating	Criteria	Reliability	Verification	Disengage Control	Consequences
O	100% OK	Current to dates	Identified & stored	Notification	Traceable data
△	1 Violation	Operators like	Current to policy	Accountable mgt.	Immediate control
X	>1 Violation	Bypass control	Run to schedule	Control actions	Strict disposition

Figure 9.4   Device confirmation matrix.

The most effective quality staffs are deeply rooted in problem prevention activities. And in the error-proofing arena, the quality staff needs a tool to continuously check the health of the error-proofing devices. Depending on your staffing level, the device evaluation matrix as shown in Figure 9.4 is a convenient way to check the health of each device and take action, as appropriate.

At most production operations, devices are checked twice daily. The device is tested with a specially controlled part that contains the given defect to make sure the device is up and running the way it should. This is an excellent practice because this twice-daily check identifies any errors in devices and help keeps them in tune. Making twice-daily checks like this is a minimal requirement for any operation and can be done by line associates at the start of the shift and right after lunch. ***Note:*** you may hear all kinds of terms for this activity, terms like *running red rabbits,* because devices are like greyhound race dogs that chase the rabbit around a track, and the "bad" part used for testing is often painted red because it has a known defect in it. You may also hear the terms *run the golden samples,* the *error-proofing dogs,* and so on, all of which suggest that the device is looking for something special.

However, in addition to this twice-daily check, it is extremely useful to have an independent person walk the process regularly and look for the minimum level of verification as well as check the overall health of all the devices. The method involves walking the line with the device evaluation matrix recording the status using the following criteria:

Device Robustness

- Rabbits need to be regularly checked by quality control experts to make sure the rabbits accurately represent the feature the device is designed to detect.
- Operators need to be checked to make sure that they like the device and have no unaddressed concerns.
- There is no bypass potential; the parts must pass through the detection device in order to be produced.

Ongoing Device Verification

- Devices have been confirmed (rabbits are properly identified and stored).
- Confirmation devices are current to certification policies (gauge policy).
- Verification is performed to schedule.

Device Disengagement Control

- When disengagement occurs, adequate notification takes place.
- Appropriate levels of management are notified upon disengagement.
- Extra controls and required containment are deployed upon disengagement.

Consequences to Defective Parts

- As nonconforming parts are found, part level data (that is traceable to each individual part) is recorded.
- Parts are placed immediately into designated and controlled containers.
- Strict and accountable disposition occurs.

Putting it All Together in the Matrix

With this information, the device verification matrix is fairly straightforward. As the problem prevention quality staff walks through and reviews the lines, the scoring is simple:

- Circle = Every criteria is intact.
- Triangle = One criteria is being violated and action is needed.
- X = Violations on two or more (immediate management attention is needed).

Having a visual posting, one that is monitored regularly by a qualified and impartial group of problem preventers and posted in the work area, will help remind the workers that error-proofing devices are important and need to be nurtured in order to catch those errors before they happen.

Key Points

- SET compliments the proactive quality staff's efforts by providing highly effective tools to monitor some of the more critical success points.
- Great device design maximizes the control based on multiple dimensions of the devices:
  - Foundation level (100% effective and simple)
  - Strategic level (operators like them so they have high uptime and positional control)
  - Discipline level (help operators follow the perfect sequence)
  - Productivity level (fast and promote lean production and one-piece flow)
- The stairway matrix is a great means to visualize the strategic placement of error-proofing devices illustrating the relative degree of customer protection that is built into the production process.
- The device confirmation matrix shows how well the company is sustaining the investment made in its error-proofing devices.
- The forms and methods in this chapter can help quality staff move into a productive role as problem preventers.

SUCCESS EVERY TIME AS A CORPORATE-WIDE STRATEGY

Chapter 10

The Strategy Behind
Success Every Time

Success Every Time (SET) is a method that uses error-proofing devices that prevent operators from making mistakes, thereby stopping errors before they ever occur. SET is, therefore, all about prevention. Mistakes cannot happen so, as a result, there is no clean up or correction process necessary.

SET is more than just error-proofing devices, however. It is a strategy.

Every company, therefore, needs a SET strategy to make sure those processes are executed correctly.

Let's start by establishing the definition of *strategy*:

> A strategy is (1) a series of moves, (2) aimed at disrupting competitive equilibrium, and (3) re-establishing it to your advantage.

Following this model, the SET strategy involves the methodical and strategic placement of error-proofing devices, a comprehensive means to see where the need for the devices is the greatest, a measurement system to track your progress, a systematic method to rate the competency of each device as well as a production process overall, plus a method to help you maximize the return on your investments to help your operators.

Ten Steps in the SET Strategy

SET as a strategy involves a series of ten steps that disrupt the potential to allow defective parts to get to customers such that you have a quality and profitability advantage in your industry.

1. Define what SET is intended to deliver to your company.
2. Document and articulate your vision for what you want error-proofing to accomplish.
3. Create a process that stimulates appropriate device creativity and evaluation.
4. Establish a method that recognizes the operational risks and drives the implementation of the devices accordingly.
5. Seek out the needs of the various device users and evaluate the devices based on these needs.
6. Establish a method that confirms devices are working as designed.
7. Establish up front what controls are needed when the error-proofing devices are turned off, for whatever reason.
8. Define very clearly what must happen when a response or part is kicked out as an error. In other words, what is the consequence?
9. Develop a library of ideas of the best methods that solve your most common problems, with a focus on standardization for people in the future to use.
10. Measure your operation for error-proofing effectiveness and drive resources at error-proofing in a systematic way.

Each step is covered in more detail in the rest of this chapter.

As you can see, SET is more than an engineer creating a limit switch or installing a proximity sensor here or there. It's a strategy—a series of moves, one linked to the other. It's also quite easy to do. The first time we outlined SET as a strategy, Gregg Neale, an extremely optimistic teacher and quality leader, and I were working to help a hardworking and dedicated group try to figure out why the devices in their plant were not delivering the types of results they expected. The group put the devices in, spent the appropriate money, and cared about the outcome, but it just wasn't working. I remember Gregg describing the tremendous frustration of the people in the plant. "They had the passion, skills, and interest but just couldn't pull the whole thing together." By developing a SET strategy, of which error-proofing devices themselves were one component, we finally saw how to elevate the perception of error-proofing above the focus on the devices and see the relevance of the infrastructure. The critical ah-ha! moment was best described by Chris Estock, an engineering manager at Mark IV Automotive:

Error-proofing devices are like a tomato plant. You can go out and buy the best ones in the world but if you don't plant them in rich soil, and give them water and sunlight, after a while they are going to die. You can kill the plant if you are missing even one element for a sustained period of time.

Until we saw SET as an overall strategy, all we did was create devices.

Examining the Ten Steps to SET

The ten steps in employing SET at your company are covered in detail in the following sections.

Define SET at Your Company

In this step, look at SET as a strategy on how the series of moves can increase your profits. A simple example could be:

SET is a strategy for our company to achieve superior customer satisfaction by providing tools to our operators so they can only make great parts. Consider these additional tips:

- SET is a company-wide approach.
- You need systematic methods that complement and work together.
- You need a combination of tools that help operators see that they are being successful.
- You need support methods to keep tools and devices functioning as designed.

Document and Articulate Your Vision

Employees respond well when an organization has a vision for the future they understand. They need to know where management is headed. If you can paint a verbal picture of what you want SET to accomplish, along with some of the guidelines the organization will honor during the journey, most people will figure out how to alter their daily work efforts in order to deliver the results.

Your vision of SET should include absolute customer satisfaction and high corporate profitability as well. In my eyes, these are very complementary objectives but you need to be smart and strategic in order to have both.

Consider this vision statement as an example:

> *It is our vision that we can provide customers with perfect products each and every time, thereby securing our future success. To achieve our vision, we need component designs that simplify the decisions and work for our production operators. In addition, we need no-cost or low-cost devices built into our production processes that are effective in helping operators do each job exactly right. We have a vision that either we will do the job exactly right or we will stop the process and take appropriate actions so that our customers can receive only perfect parts. Through these actions we have a vision of our customers bragging to their friends and family about the products we make, creating more lifetime loyal customers for ourselves and our legacy.*

Consider these additional tips:

- Be bold and paint the most vivid and compelling dream possible.
- Include quality and cost verbiage. You want and need both.
- Start the process as a draft statement, initially created by management, and then invite the organization to participate in its refinement.
- Be patient and supportive of the organization as it learns. Believe in them, they will get there, if you are consistent.

Create Processes That Stimulate Appropriate Device Creativity and Evaluation

To succeed in your implementation of SET, two processes need to be established.

- The first is in the world of engineering, in which a structured approach is needed to analyze each operation and the design features that help operators make each part right. This engineering process needs to involve management working with engineers to study each operation and define the level of support needed.
- The second process is in the world of manufacturing. Structured methods and reviews are needed to confirm that error-proofing devices are

working properly. The confirmation process needs to include in the scope, making sure devices are working, that operators like them, and that when a device spots that needle-in-a-haystack problem part, appropriate actions are taken.

For both the engineering and the manufacturing work, management needs to establish reviews of the relevant topics and make the matter of SET a priority for the company. Simplicity in error-proofing devices is better than complexity. Creative engineers often enjoy jumping to a complex, high-tech solution that costs more than you need to spend. Always think "creativity before capital." You want your engineers to find the least expensive and most effective solutions possible. A great example is the gas-cap strap. The strap costs less than a penny but it prevents you from leaving the cap at the gas station (or on top of your car) and avoids a potential fire hazard.

For your company to excel, you also need a systematic rating and evaluation process that drives creativity before complexity and capital. Refer back to the rating matrices shown in Chapters 4, 5, and 6 (Figures 4.4, 5.3, and 6.3). They place a premium on ideal controls, with a bias toward simplicity and low cost.

Consider these additional tips:

- Have your engineers share ideas and brainstorm best practices and devices.
- Include in the device identification supplier of poke-yoke devices.
- Seek the ideas of your operators; they know what works.
- Put in place a structured evaluation system.
- Include in the evaluation a bias to use known and proven solutions.

Establish a Method That Recognizes the Operational Risks and Drives the Implementation of the Devices Accordingly

Not all operations and processes are created equally; there are different levels of risks based on your business environment. Generally speaking, the categories of the greatest risk include the following and indicate where you want to place error-proofing devices:

- **Points of customer use:** If you buy a cell phone and the on/off button does not work, all the other features are meaningless.
- **Areas of high scrap:** You are in a competitive business, and scrap means lost profits. Placing devices to help high-scrap processes is just plain smart.

- **Safety and regulatory:** Do not let people get hurt and don't violate regulations.
- **High warranty concerns:** You can't stop physics. Points of high friction and high loads fail first and drive up warranty costs. Place devices here.
- **The last operations on any line:** In most plants, downstream operators check the work of upstream operators. Something will look different, and the operators cull those "different looking" parts out. But your last operators on any line have only the customers behind them. If the last operator makes a mistake, only the customer can find the defect.

Consider these additional tips:

- Recognize that every business has operations with different risks.
- Articulate the risks that are most significant to your business success.
- Drive extra effort and support to the items with the highest risk.
- In every business, the operations closest to the customers have maximum risk. Your last operator is the riskiest because only your customer can discover mistakes of your last operator. Place maximum priority on your last operations.

Seek Out the Needs of Various Device Users and Evaluate Devices Based on These Needs

In most businesses, production operators succeed most of the time. In the auto industry, for example, the rate of defective parts is usually under 200 defective parts per million (PPM) produced. This means production operators are 99.98% successful and have defects at a rate of 2 out of 10,000. SET is seeking ways to eliminate these 2 defects from reaching a customer. Operators will welcome devices that can pick out the 2 defects, but they don't want extra work on the 9,998 cycles where they are already doing the work correctly. You want to make the process better and easier for them with error-proofing devices that they like to use and that make their jobs easier, not harder. Keep in mind, too, that operators are not all alike. You have tall and short operators, men and women, operators who are right handed and left handed. Make sure your devices work for operators of all shapes, sizes, and characteristics.

Consider these additional tips:

- Recognize your operators don't want uncomfortable work.
- Design devices with the realization that operator discomfort with devices is usually related to physical characteristics of operators.
- Establish a cross section of the workforce that represents a wide variety of sizes and characteristics and have the operators evaluate the devices under a controlled situation.
- If operators have concerns, address them in a way that all operators will welcome the devices.

Establish a Method That Confirms Devices Are Working as Designed

Businesses and production activities are dynamic—change is the only constant. SET is built upon a strategy that places cost-effective error-proofing devices into your operation, and these devices need to work as they were designed to work. You need to take an active and systematic approach that confirms the methods you have in place are constantly functioning as designed. One of the worst possible scenarios you can have is to allow your devices—which are designed to protect your reputation with your customer—to go out of control and stay that way. You would have been smarter not to invest in the device in the first place. Establish methods to ensure that devices are working as intended, as described in Chapter 9.

Consider these additional tips:

- Design methods for your quality staff to systematically confirm the proper functioning or all success-related devices.
- Hold your quality staff accountable for protecting customers from errors.
- Recognize the SET is truly a problem prevention activity.

Establish What Controls Are Needed When the Error-Proofing Devices Are Turned Off

There will be situations when the error-proofing devices need to be disengaged (such as when a design change needs to be rushed into a part or when a device is malfunctioning and is identifying good parts as defective), and your company will be relying on the operators to run without built-in support. There will also be times when you discover a device is not working properly, and your customer has been placed at risk. During these situations, your company needs an easy to implement set of actions to back the production operators up. The most obvious process is some type of increased level of inspection. When these situations occur, the management team needs to put in place a process to make the vulnerability of a disengaged device visible to the team and to require an appropriate level of customer protection control. For example, if the device is malfunctioning and you need to turn it off, put a redundant inspection in place to protect your customer until a properly functioning device is restored.

Consider these additional tips:

- Make the device disengagement visible to the entire team.
- Take action to implement a cost-effective method to protect your customer.
- Re-establish systematic error-proofing control as quickly as possible.

Define Clearly What Must Happen When a Bad Part Is Identified

When you don't control parts kicked out of the process for being out of specification or containing some other mistake or defect, you may have non-conforming parts escaping to your customers.

What tends to happen is that when a part contains a defect and the system kicks it out (that is, the part isn't allowed it to continue along the production line), the part has to be repaired or discarded. If the repair person looks at the part, imposes personal judgment, and determines that the part was good, that bad part will end up in the hands of the customer. You have lost on every possible count, including a possible warranty cost in addition to the customer dissatisfaction. Yet the repair person who makes this type of mistake is probably trying to be cost conscious and help the company.

The SET strategy needs clearly defined consequences for kicked-out parts. The company needs a plan to handle the proper marking and identification of each substandard part as well as marking the defects related to each part. If rework is allowed, it must be complete and total. The entire SET strategy can become a complete waste if the consequences to the parts are improperly defined.

Consider these additional tips:

- Recognize that controlling the parts kicked out of the process is a hugely precious element. You have invested in a system that does not allow these parts to continue along the production line, and the worst scenario that could happen is that your customer receives these known bad parts.

■ Understand that operators who let the defective parts escape are probably trying to help the company save some money, yet their efforts created the greatest loss possible.

■ Have a very structured and disciplined plan to monitor and control these parts, including marking the parts and the associated defects.

Develop a Library of Ideas with a Focus on Standardization

The most successful companies have an ability to copy the best practices and standardize as much as possible. In simple terms, they capture the best ideas and share them across the organization—they have a *library* of great ideas. Especially with the devices, such a library can simplify implementation because people can become familiar with the characteristics of devices. Capturing this information into a library and making it available across the company creates leverage and profits.

Consider these additional tips:

■ Identify a person or staff who can filter the ideas and keep track of the best.

■ Create a sharable inventory of knowledge.

■ Try to establish a standard set of devices that work in many areas of the company.

Measure Your Operation for Error-Proofing Effectiveness and Drive Resources at Error-Proofing in a Systematic Way

What you measure is typically what you get. A SET metric system includes:

■ A concise method to rate each operation (see Chapters 4, 5, and 6) for the strength of controls at the part level, the set-up level, and the parameter level.

■ A routine method to confirm the devices and support systems are working as designed (see Chapter 9 for details).

■ An organization that can respond when management reviews these aspects on a regular basis.

Consider these additional tips:

■ The SET process is built around systematically ratings both devices and operations to allow management to see the robustness of the production system.

■ Establish the quality staff as the champions of the SET system.

Key Points

■ SET is a strategy that goes beyond just designing error-proofing devices. The strategy involves ten steps.

■ When your operators can only succeed, you have created the greatest process in any industry because your customers are totally protected.

■ Your customers judge you based on the products they get—good or bad. Your reputation and long-term success is based on what your operators deliver.

Chapter 11

Putting it All Together

The Success Every Time (SET) method is a great addition to the quality world, but you cannot stop there. This focus on error-proofing is a cultural activity that requires multiple parts of the organization to get involved. All departments and areas need to understand this is not a "plant thing." It is not just manufacturing's project, or quality's or engineering's. It's company-wide, and everyone has a role.

The scope of the total effort spans the cradle-to-grave nature of production. At the start, you have the engineering efforts that drive what the customers receive. The main portion of your success comes in the months and years of making and selling products. During this entire process learning takes place, and the greatest companies have methods to constantly build their knowledge base and turn lessons into competitive advantage. SET views this learning as a key part of the continuous improvement system, especially when you can put it all together.

SET is a Team Sport

Everyone in your company needs to cooperate in order to help the company be error-free. This is not just a manufacturing or a quality thing. SET is a company thing, a mindset. When you look at error-proofing in that way, everyone has a role.

SET starts with design. The best designs have features that allow the parts to fit together easily and also include unique physical identifying features that help operators select the exact right part for each job. Simply stated, this means there are no look-alike parts. Design engineers can also make production easier by including discrete markings on each part so operators can confirm they have done the operation correctly. Small dots or lines on mating parts that show operators they have completed the proper alignment are a simple and inexpensive means to error-proof.

SET practitioners from other staffs play significant roles as well. The finance staff needs to understand the total cost of errors and provide the economic justification to place error-proofing devices in ideal locations, especially when spending a little more money upfront provides significant profits later on. Purchasing has a role to make sure the equipment specifications have error-proofing devices included. Purchasing also needs to push your suppliers to include SET devices in their processes as well. Human resources staff needs to train the operators on the value of the devices, helping operators understand the overall strategy in order to maximize your potential.

Product Engineering

Each individual part needs a distinct and unique identifier. To maximize the benefits, product engineering needs to use physical interference devices to help operators always select the right parts and position them perfectly. If parts are designed with unique tabs, holes, and shapes that the operators can utilize, simple devices can be deployed that work successfully all the time, with minimal cost and maintenance.

Purchasing

Purchasing has two roles. First, SET needs to permeate the supply chain, with each supplier following a similar method. If your production is error-proofed but the supply chain has holes, your products are vulnerable to the supply chain weaknesses—remember that your customer does not care if the defect came from you or from your suppliers, so your reputation is at risk if your suppliers aren't error-proofed. It's your responsibility to protect the customer from supplier issues.

The second role for purchasing is securing proper parameter controls in the machinery and equipment they buy. The parameter monitoring section of the SET approach needs simple and effective sensing devices built into this equipment. Providing these features has to be built into the purchasing process. The purchasing specifications for the equipment need to have specifications for the monitoring devices to be built in.

Finance

The SET process can ultimately save a lot of money and needs to be recognized for the value it can bring to the company. When operators are not making mistakes, yields rise. There is less scrap, and machines have more available capacity, which means they can be deployed for other profitable means. With fewer errors, there will be fewer customer complaints, claims, and ill will from customers. If a sensing device is available and needs some funding, the finance staff needs to recognize the value of problem prevention. At the same time, the finance staff needs to be careful about encouraging spending huge funds for highly sophisticated devices. The use of such sophisticated devices should be rare, although there may be times that high-tech equipment is appropriate and needed. In such cases, the finance staff needs to support the expenditures and the staff to keep those sophisticated devices running properly.

Manufacturing/Process/Industrial Engineering

Manufacturing engineering is where the heart of the error-proofing process comes alive. Manufacturing engineers have to come up with the clever devices that help operators succeed, and with minimal cost and maximum precision. The imagination of the engineers will be taxed, but their creativity and ideas can carry the company to new levels of execution, especially when the devices are appreciated by the operators and can keep up with production rates.

Information Technology

Manufacturing engineers will be coming up with some great ideas, but they need both a place to store the knowledge and an easy way to catalogue the devices. When an engineer or engineering team invents a good idea, a lessons-learned file is the best way to store it and keep it available for use. Computers excel in this role and need to be made available with simple methods to store the data and devices based on key actions and devices. There are a lot of quality systems providers (IQS of Rocky River, Ohio, comes to mind) offering integrated file structures that can help engineers link the various knowledge stores and make them easily retrievable. John Cachat of IQS described the error-proofing device information system in this way: "Systems need to provide a place for the knowledge to be stored and then have a fast and integrated means to bring the essential information back to the engineer, making him more successful"; great information.

Quality Staff

Quality staff has the responsibility to keep the total quality system functioning as designed. Most people realize and understand the quality staff's responsibility to represent the customer and provide the service to continuously check parts. As part of that job, the quality staff provides objective information on how good the production parts are. They look at parts and compare them to specifications and make decisions of good versus bad. This customer protection aspect is one level of the quality staff's function. A second level is that the quality staff defines the strategic points in the production process where quality checks are performed. Within this activity, the quality staff typically determines the degree of inspection needed at each control point.

However, the best way is for a quality staff to be engaged in managing the quality system. At this level, the quality staff is actively engaged in confirming the activities that create quality are functioning properly, consistently, and as intended. In this effort, they confirm that the ingredients for SET are present and honored. The quality staff also must verify that a bad part is rejected in some way; that is, that the defective part is managed such that customers only receive great parts.

Quality Control Staff

Most quality control staff members fall into two categories: problem solvers and problem preventers. Unfortunately, problem solvers tend to dominate the staff in terms of activity and notoriety. These are the brave firefighters who step in when there is a problem, and they work tirelessly to fix it. In an industrial setting, problem solvers are the ones who go to disappointed or irate customers and provide the great recovery story to restore the company's reputation. They take the beatings for the firm and do a great job in returning the process to stability. Because of these high visibility efforts, they deserve and receive a lot of recognition and often are the ones promoted to management due to their accomplishments and dedication. They are good people.

The problem is that they need problems in order to shine. With problems, they can show their skills under immense pressure. Without the problems or pressures, the problem solver has no arena.

Management

Management needs to understand that its role to help the organization make tasks easier for the operator. If management is not focused on helping the operators by having all functional staffs make the work of the production operators easier, it's time to learn and internalize some new behaviors. Management has the responsibility to define what these new actions are and then help the organization create the new behaviors around those actions. The entire company has to view the 100% success of production operators as the most important priority of the entire company because the output of the production operators is what the customers receive. Your entire reputation in the marketplace is determined by how your customers evaluate your products. Bad products mean a bad reputation. Great products mean you have earned the trust of your customers. In order to excel, management must provide a system that identifies what your production operators need in order to be successful every time and follow through by satisfying operator needs in a timely manner.

Let me provide some examples. If the people in product design are allowed to release multiple designs for parts with the same function, without a conscious effort to consolidate the designs, the product engineers make the part selection process more difficult for operators. Have you ever had to replace the battery in your watch and went to the store for a replacement? The first problem you encounter is an assortment of battery styles, each one slightly different from the other. Your decision on which battery to use is made tougher due to the number of manufacturers you can choose from, each with a different battery numbering system. It would be easier if you only had a few sizes to choose from, similar to the AAA/AA/C/D sized batteries for flashlights and radios. Watch battery designers could also simplify the selection process by having a color code or marking symbol on the battery. If your watch has a battery with a certain mark (like a diamond or a star), you could look at the battery choices and match the symbols to help you choose the proper one. That symbol would be a built-in indicator that helps you as the watch battery replacement operator.

Management needs to drive all the functional staff to include methods like these to help operators succeed.

Production Operators

Operators are critical to the deployment of SET. Operators are the ones who create the value for customers to enjoy. When they succeed, the company succeeds. Operators need simple and effective devices that help them do the job correctly every time, with no burdensome work. If they don't get the proper devices, it is incumbent on the operators to come up with suggestions.

Operators are the ones who get criticized for producing defective products, so they have the right to push for the devices they need.

The Two Phases of Error-Proofing Deployment

In the production phase, people need to make sure devices are working properly and, as issues arise, the concept of SET is built into the problem-solving process. In the planning phase, people need to take the best ideas and roll the concepts into the design of the parts and process.

In the SET process, the activities done early in the design phase are different from the key activities that need to be done during production. Therefore, the actions to address error-proofing are split into two phases: improve current production and product design and planning.

Process Engineering (Production Phase) versus Product Engineering (Planning Phase)

The necessity of these structured roles and responsibilities of the error-proofing system was best described by Roger Ruggiero (a retired vice president of automotive manufacturing) who was discussing how the Japanese, specifically Toyota, look at producing cars. Roger was describing how the design of the parts and the design of the process are harmonious, and how each of the design elements were aimed at making the task of the operator easy.

- The *product engineer* has the responsibility to create a design that provides the necessary function at the lowest cost and must execute the design in such a manner that it is easy to make.
- The *process engineer* needs to find ideal methods to reduce operating variation relative to the part and make the process safe and efficient for the operators. These engineers have to find the devices to maximize the likelihood of success. The keys for the process engineer are a combination of features within the parts themselves as well as features within the tools and equipment. Process engineers have the responsibility of blending the features of the part with the nuances of the tooling and equipment.

Starting with Production

Logic would tell you that the start of the SET process should begin in the design phase. From a purist's point of view, this logic is solid and sound. Unfortunately, it is almost impossible to predict how well a production line or area will flow despite our best efforts.

Instead, I take the opposite view (the pragmatist's point of view), which is to start with the problems and successes of today. There is immense knowledge in your own factories and in other companies. People know what works, they know how friendly and effective each device is, and they know what does not work.

I believe you need to start SET implementation by jumping right into the production phase and looking for success-generating opportunities there. I realize all the constraints of money, timing, tooling, and all the rest. And, yes, installing error-proofing devices in an after-the-fact manner is never easy. If you had a clean sheet of paper, installing the devices into the system would be much easier and less expensive. I completely and totally realize this. Regardless, I still think you need to start with production, not with product planning. The "Ten Reasons to Start the Error-Proofing Process During the Production Phase" sidebar gives you a close look at why.

Ten Reasons to Start the Error-Proofing Process During the Production Phase

- The issues of today are causing real scrap and real customer complaints.
- The process flaws that were not evident in the planning phase are now visible.
- Operators can tell you precisely what they do and don't like.
- Operators can tell you what should work, what won't work, and why!
- You can learn from devices that are being underutilized.
- When obstacles occur, you will be pushed to be creative, and get good ideas.
- The organization can rally to help because profitability is being hurt . . . today.
- Issue visibility and resolution will motivate prevention (that is, the pain is real).
- The role of everyone is easier to understand when you don't have something and need it.
- Eliminating today's problems maximizes your immediate results; you get stronger, faster.

When you start your error-proofing process in the production phase, you see the relevance of the "realness of production." Operators can tell you what works and what doesn't because it is real. You will be working with actual problems, saving actual scrap, and saving actual money. You will also have to confront the real limitations of money and space and a whole host of other constraints. Although these challenges are frustrating, they will also motivate you to be more creative, brainstorming twenty or thirty ideas that really work, that operators like, and that are inexpensive. All of this is good for your company. You will also find a set of devices that really work and create the foundation of a standardized set of devices that fit your needs and serve you well. You are creating knowledge.

Problem Solving on the Production Floor

There are always production problems, and there probably always will be production problems. Even with the SET process, there will be problems. SET has the capacity to significantly reduce problems and keep them from escaping to customers, but it probably cannot eliminate every problem. A concept I learned while working for Toyota at the NUMMI plant in Fremont, California, was "problem solving is the key to success." You always will have problems and they come in two types: the first, problems you don't want, where things are not going to plan. This is reactive problem solving and it must get the first priority, to get things stable. The second, problems you create for yourself, looking for new ways to achieve a higher standard or achieving what currently cannot be done and reach new heights.

Solving problems is the best way to retain what is working and take you to new and better heights. Effective problem solving is based in pragmatism; it is based in reality. The Japanese problem solve better than anyone else because they have a habit of sticking with what works and trying new methods out in a small-scale, controlled environment. When the new idea is proven to work, they copy it wherever practical.

For this reason, if you are starting a SET process, I encourage you to begin your SET activity by looking at your current process and reacting to the shortcomings you find. By improving your processes using SET, you will learn the most efficient methods of implementation. The advantage you can then create is using the structured approach of all elements of SET. You can also do a much better job of preventing problems before production starts. Please review the proactive reactive activities shown in Figure 11.1.

Figure 11.1 is a universal diagram of a basic system illustrating how inputs are converted by a process to achieve results and the management interaction to drive resources for continuous improvements. Let me give you an example of a system. My wife, Cindy, makes fabulous chocolate chip cookies, and she has a system that makes her cookies the best. The first part of her system is the inputs of the ingredients and her recipe. She selects the right type and quantity of sugar; she uses the best flour, eggs, butter, and chocolate chips. Next, she goes into the conversion process of mixing the ingredients in a certain order before she puts them on the cookie sheet to place them in the oven.

Cindy uses the management review system as well because she looks at the final product and keeps track of how long to bake each tray in order to achieve the correct softness and chewiness. She will make adjustments as

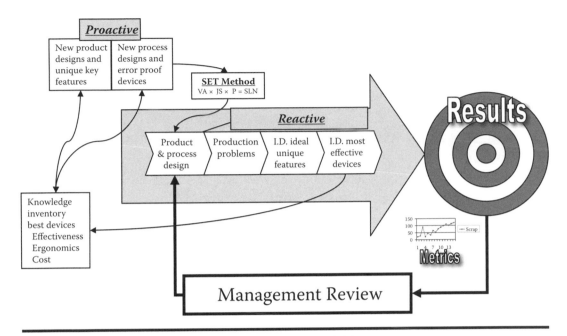

Figure 11.1 SET system proactive and reactive activities.

needed, which is her management review process and resource redeployment activity. Just like in Figure 11.1, she has a closed loop system to make cookies and her cookies are great.

The same thing goes for SET. It needs to be viewed as a system. The inputs are the part specifications and the processes needed to make great products. The conversion processes are the activities to design and rate each device to help operators win. Finally, management reviews are needed to drive continuous improvement.

For companies that have the passion to be the best, extending problem solving into error-proofing is a natural process that includes the following basic steps:

1. The problem is identified and containment is instituted as needed.
2. Analysis of the problem is based on sound logic and effective use of data.
3. A root cause is identified (confirmed by turning the problem on and off).
4. Solution alternatives are identified and evaluated, including error-proofing. Error-proofing lessons learned are reviewed for duplication, and new error-proofing ideas are included in a lessons-learned inventory.
5. For customer-discovered issues, the detection system receives equal analysis.

6. Once implemented, device evaluation and verification is put into effect to confirm the effectiveness.
7. Lessons-learned documentation is finalized.
8. Duplication of the solution is sought in other areas of the plant.

In his book *The Toyota Way,* Jeffrey Liker describes the premium Toyota places on problem solving. They see their employees as a font of knowledge in terms of what is really happening in the manufacturing, assembly, or service process. Toyota wants its people always looking at problems as opportunities to fuel continuous improvement, and they work very hard to help their people solve problems. Error-proofing is a natural step for them because it is a core method to identify and eliminate waste. Driving error-proofing into problem solving just makes sense.

Getting Started on the Plant Floor

One of the powerful secrets to effective error-proofing is to conduct a systematic review of your existing devices and determine whether they are being effectively deployed and supported (see the discussion in Chapter 9 of the device confirmation matrix). You need a small task force to comb through the plant and look at each station from the operators' points of view, see what is there, and determine whether it is working properly.

This task force needs to understand that they are just reviewing the devices, seeing how well they are working, and serving the people on the floor. Much more important are the side benefits that the organization will derive, such as the following:

- All the devices will be up and functional.
- Operators will have a greater appreciation for the value of the devices.
- The reviewers will be able to identify the types of devices that work best.
- The task force can consolidate your lessons learned.

Creating a library of knowledge is the starting point of a lessons-learned file. You have a set of people with knowledge of what works on the production floor (and why it works), including specific examples of the devices in operation. Most organizations have their own way of capturing the lessons into a file. If you don't, consider expanding the device evaluation matrix by adding a few columns for more data, including

- A small photo of the device.
- A description of the device, based on the foundation rating in the SET device matrix (see Chapter 4).
- Operations information (site location, part, etc.).
- Device technical information (model numbers and supplier).
- Name of the expert (process engineer, supervisor, etc.).
- Type of reminder provided (select correct part, placement, processing, etc.).

This core data is the starting point of an effective lessons-learned inventory. It is based on real information with real operator comments and real solutions. All of this is coming from the task force, which is helping you achieve stability, saving a tremendous amount of money, and improving your reputation in the eyes of customers.

Upfront Planning

In the world of the product design engineer, great pains are taken to come up with designs that meet functional requirements. If you're designing a toaster, for example, you're thinking about how fast the coils heat up, how to get the spring to release the toast at the right time, and so forth. As the design evolves, engineers will frequently identify some of the more critical aspects of the design and emphasize them as key control characteristics or other special characteristics because they know these elements have a significant impact on the overall product. Design for six sigma, design for manufacturability, and design for assembly, and other similar processes are aimed at reducing complexity in order to give customers a great product. The essential goal is a robust design. Unfortunately, most of these efforts stop one step short of incorporating error-proofing in a structured manner.

However, there needs to be another element that we are overlooking, features that the manufacturing engineer and the manufacturing people can emphasize in order to be successful on each and every part made. The Japanese excel at this. They take the time to build into the design a small set of enablers that make the production job easier. These features must have greater significance than the set of special controls or key product characteristics. This is because these features establish production stability, and with a stable process, you can improve almost anything. When you build key identifying features into the parts, the manufacturing/process engineers have a much easier job.

Product development processes to build in a unique feature on each part—a feature approved by the manufacturing engineers—as a reference point for the SET process to work. In fact, management must mandate that error-proofing features are required before the part or design can be released into production. The product design engineer's work is not complete until these features are in place.

Key Points

- SET is not just a production floor thing; it is a strategy for success in the marketplace that requires the involvement of every functional staff.
- Management's role is to drive the functional areas to help operators succeed on each and every part they make.
- Companies employing SET should have all their people recognize the following:
  - Your customers evaluate your company based on the products they receive—good products mean a good reputation; bad products mean a bad reputation
  - The output of your production operators is what your customers receive
  - To win in the marketplace, all staff must focus on helping your operators succeed on each and every part they make
- The best role of the quality staff is to improve the system of quality.
- View the SET activities as a closed-loop system.
- Start your improvement process by improving your current production process. You will see immediate gains. You will obtain deeper knowledge on the practical activities that work.
- Capture your knowledge as lessons learned and drive it into your upfront design efforts as soon as possible.

Selected Readings

Altshuller, Genrich. *40 Principles: TRIZ Keys to Technical Innovation.* Worchester, MA: Technical Innovation Center, 2002.

Anderson, Bjorn, and Tom Fagerhaug. *Root Cause Analysis.* Milwaukee, WI: ASQ Quality Press, 2000.

Bossidy, Larry, and Ram Chrah. *Execution.* New York: Crown Business, 2002.

Crosby, Philip B. *Quality Is Free.* New York: McGraw-Hill, 1979.

———. *Quality Without Tears.* New York: McGraw-Hill, 1984.

Deming, W. Edward. *Out of the Crisis.* Cambridge: Massachusetts Institute of Technology, 1982.

Goldsmith, Marshall. *What Got You Here Won't Get You There.* New York: Hyperion, 2007.

Hinckley, Martin C. *Make No Mistake!* Portland, OR: Productivity Press, 2001.

Koch, Richard. *The 80/20 Principle.* New York: Bantam Doubleday Dell, 1998.

Liker, Jeffrey K. *The Toyota Way.* New York: McGraw-Hill, 2004.

Liker, Jeffrey K., and David Meier. *The Toyota Way Fieldbook.* New York: McGraw-Hill, 2006.

Lowe, Janet. *Jack Welch Speaks.* New York: Wiley, 1998.

Musashi, Miyamoto. *A Book of Five Rings.* Woodstock, NY: Overlook Press, 1982.

Nikkan Kogyo Shimbun, Ltd. *Poke-Yoke.* Portland, OR: Productivity Press, 1988.

Pitano, Rick. *Success Is a Choice.* New York: Broadway Books, 1977.

Trout, Jack. *The Power of Simplicity.* New York: McGraw-Hill, 1999.

Womack, James., and Jones, Daniel T. *Lean Thinking,* New York, Free Press, 1996.

About the Author

John Casey is a strategic thinker with a definite bias toward thinking outside the box. His career includes assignments in a wide cross-section of business functions, including manufacturing, purchasing, quality, finance, and manufacturing engineering. John's business perspective and approach were shaped during his three-year assignment working for Toyota at New United Motor Manufacturing Incorporated (NUMMI), as part of Toyota's joint venture with General Motors in Fremont, California. At NUMMI, John was the program manager for the launch of the Corolla and Prizm car models.

In addition, John served as the director of General Motors' North American Supplier Quality, the director of Purchasing and Supplier Quality for the Cadillac Luxury Car Division, and the Chrysler director of the Quality Assurance and Audit Team (a supplier development staff).

John's career has been spent mostly in the auto industry, and he has been active in industry-wide efforts. He has been a member of the Board of Directors of the Automotive Industry Action Group (AiAG), is a past chairman of the AiAG Quality Steering Committee, and has held multiple chairman positions of different AiAG project teams. John is also a member of the American Society for Quality (ASQ) and served as the 2008–2009 Chairman of the ASQ Automotive Section.

John was awarded a fellowship and earned an MBA from the University of Michigan as well as a BS from General Motors Institute (now called Kettering University).

Index

A

Auto industry suppliers, performance of, 3
Automatic teller machine, 11

B

Bad part control, 86–93
Bad product creation, 9

C

Controlled disengagement, 83
Critical few, 6

D

Device(s)
 compatibility, 71–74
 confirmation matrix, 100–103
 designing great, 95–97
 disengagement control, 83–85, 102
 error proofing, 8–15, 113
  confirmation matrix for, 100–103
  disengagement of, 113–114
  evaluation of, 112–113
  features of best, 13–14
  mistake proofing devices *vs.,* 11–12
  placement of, 111–112
  point of recognition, 11
  recognizing true, 12–13
  in specific areas, 14–15
  stairway matrix for, 98–99
  type of control, 11
 investing in, 75–94
 library, 115
 ongoing verification, 102

operator friendliness, 78–81
 form evaluation of, 80
 robustness, 75–81
 special characteristics, 71
 support mechanisms, 76

E

Error proofing
 deployment, 122–127
 devices, 8–15, 40–41, 113
  confirmation matrix for, 100–103
  disengagement of, 113–114
  evaluation of, 112–113
  features of best, 13–14
  mistake proofing devices *vs.,* 11–12
  placement of, 111–112
  point of recognition, 11
  recognizing true, 12–13
  in specific areas, 14–15
  stairway matrix for, 98–99
  type of control, 11
 effectiveness, 115–116
 key, 14
 mistake proofing *vs.,* 8–15
 positioning, 12
 in set-up levels, 55–58
 two phases of deployment, 122
Error-proofing dogs, 102

F

Failure Mode Effects Analysis (FMEA), 3
 bias toward high severity, 5–6
 detection capability, 4
 elements of risk, 4–5
 ever-increasing opportunity, 6